LARA ANNIBOLETTI

79 STORIES ABOUT POMPEII
that no one ever told you...

«L'ERMA» di BRETSCHNEIDER

Lara Anniboletti

79 stories about Pompeii
that no one ever told you...

«L'ERMA» di BRETSCHNEIDER

Editorial Director
Roberto Marcucci

Editors
Elena Montani
Maurizio Pinto
Dario Scianetti

Editorial secretary
Alessia Francescangeli

Graphic design, layout, image processing
Maurizio Pinto

Cover
Maurizio Pinto

si ringrazia
l'Ing. Giuseppe Barbella per l'elaborazione grafica della mappa.

Lara Anniboletti

79 stories about Pompeii. That no one ever told you ... / Lara Anniboletti -
Roma : «L'ERMA» di BRETSCHNEIDER, 148 p. : ill.; 24 cm. -

ISBN 978-88-913-1654-7 (paperback)
ISBN 978-88-913-1655-4 (pdf)

CDD 930.10240544

1. Pompei

"For Jacopo and Greta"

Table of contents

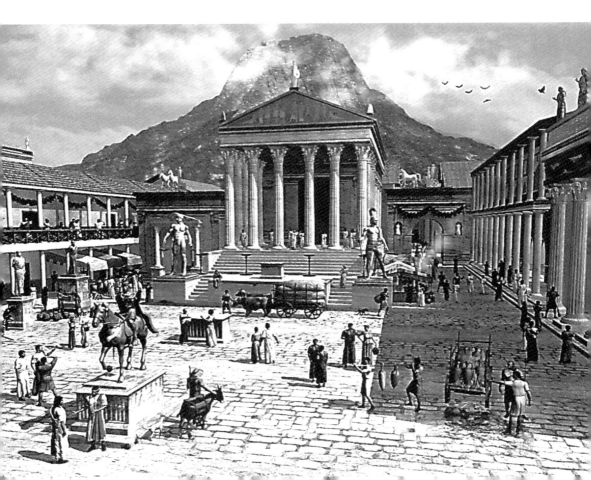

Foreword

Now a highly sought after modern travel destination, since the 18th century, the Gulf of Naples and its antiquities have been one of the favorite choices of artists, intellectuals, and scholars fascinated by the extraordinary mix of nature and history, recognizing the art of the land and finding nostalgia in a lost paradise. Even today, Pompeii, with its lifestyle and settlements interrupted by the eruption in 79 AD and then again with this "second life" that began with excavations in 1748, does not cease to fascinate, intrigue, attract and inspire travelers, artists and ever-increasing numbers of tourists (this year alone more than 3,000,000 people have visited).

Lara Anniboletti's book is part of the fertile grove of publications dedicated to Pompeii, intended to tell Pompeii's story and inform people about the city who, inspired by the direct testimony of a way of life from 2000 years ago that is here so remarkably perceptible, come to Pompeii to feed their imagination and feelings, along with their intellect. It is a book that can be placed in the category of exceptional "one of a kind" guides such as Amedeo Maiuri's *"Pompei ed Ercolano tra case ed abitanti"* written in 1958 with the declared intention that "in those houses that were 'still warm with humanity', an archaeologist could find their favorite type of place, bending over to read the thousands of hidden signs, a scholar committed to giving a spark of life back to the rooms and characters..."

The encounter between archaeological knowledge and literary creativity was what brought about these 79 stories about Pompeii, anecdotes and curiosities that have come about during 200 years of digging, fragments of the life of people from the time that the imagination then animates, returning them to their historical dimension. Pompeii resurfaces from the oblivion of centuries and on its streets, you can meet Caecilius Jucundus, the banker, and Julia Felix, the cunning matron. The barber Faventinus was shaving his morning beard and an unlucky patron at Salvius's workshop was the victim of swindling while gambling at dice, while the smells from Modesto's bakery fill the air once more, just as the cries of the town crier, the voices of merchants in the Forum, and the noise of the horses' hoofs on the streets.

The balance that mixes science with fun in these stories is capable of transporting the reader into a communicative sphere in which the didactic intent is almost imperceptible, even though it underlies the entire narrative. It is a significant starting point for a much needed sharing of archaeological information, adapted to the demands of an ever-growing and hard to please audience.

MASSIMO OSANNA
General Director of Pompeii's Archaeological Park

1. What was Vesuvius like before the eruption?

Vesuvius' distinctive outline in the background of the Forum of Pompeii is the most common image found on the covers of the

city's tourist guides. Anyone who has ever visited Pompeii has looked up at least once to admire it. But not everyone knows that, in the eyes of a Pompeian who looked towards the Temple of Jupiter, Mt. Vesuvius did not look like it does today. It was much more impressive and had the conical-shaped point of a real volcano! Vesuvius' current outline is the result of the terrible eruption that occurred at 1 pm on August 24th, 79 AD when the "lava plug" that was holding the top of the volcano closed was forced open by strong pressure from underlying gases. The violent explosion projected a column of ashes, gas, and fragments of lava straight up into the air for more than 14 km above Vesuvius before falling to the ground, producing a downpour of volcanic material. Pompeii was buried under a thick coat of ash in some places up to 7 meters deep! This ash layer was the ultimate cause of the deaths of everyone who had stayed hidden inside their homes in the city instead of fleeing. They died from inhaling deadly fumes or were trapped by the collapse of buildings caused by the weight of the pumice and frequent earthquakes. In the 44 hectares of land that have been excavated, the bodies of 1150 victims have been found, which, together with 258 others found in the suburbs, added up to a tragedy: in an estimated population of about 20,000 inhabitants, the death toll was more than 15%!

2. What happened afterwards?

We all know what happened during the eruption of Vesuvius ... but what about after? What was it like?

The eruption that destroyed Pompeii and the other centers around Vesuvius came as a complete surprise to the ancient Pompeiians who had long ignored the volcanic nature of the mountain, famous for its lush vineyards. The disastrous earthquake of February 5, 62 AD, estimated at around 8.0 on the Richter Scale, and a series of aftershocks also measuring 3.0 to 5.0 in magnitude had shaken the area in the decades before the catastrophe, but no one had linked the events with the presence of the volcano or ever imagined the imminent disaster. Immediately after the eruption, the Roman Emperor Titus attempted to organize the first rescue efforts for the affected areas by sending an Impe-rial commission to assess the damage and salvage as much as possible. Private citizens dug tunnels beneath the hardened lava and made holes into the walls of houses to retrieve precious objects, their loved ones' bodies and whatever furnishings were still useable. These activities continued until the following year when the Emperor visited the area and decided that any attempt to restore life to the buried cities was in vain. Pompeii remained a vague reference on Roman maps until the Middle Ages, when even the name was then forgotten. The area where the town had been became known as "City Hill" and from there, news occasionally circulated of random discoveries.

3. A strange news story from ancient times

Have you ever wondered why today, 2000 years later, we are able to reconstruct with such journalistic precision the news story from the day of the eruption at Pompeii?

At that time, there were no newspapers or national newscasts. The eruption in 79 AD is without a doubt the most famous volcanic eruption in history as a result of the accounts of the direct experience of a young patrician of the time, Pliny the Younger, which have survived and been passed on to us. 25 years after the incident, Pliny sent two letters to the famous historian *Tacitus* in which he recounted the catastrophe and described the death of his uncle, the famous naturalist Pliny the Elder. The latter gave his name to the term "Plinian eruption" which today is used to describe explosive volcanic activity similar to the Mt. Vesuvius eruption.

In order to go and observe the strange phenomenon that was happening and help the affected population, Pliny the Elder had set off in the direction of Pompeii from Capo Miseno, near Pozzuoli, where he lived as commander of the Imperial fleet of Rome. Given that it was impossible to stay in the city, Pliny took refuge at the villa of his friend *Pomponianus* near *Stabiae*, where he spent the night. The next day, the group, protecting their heads from the falling pumice with pillows, tried to escape, but Pliny, poisoned by the gases, was struck with a sudden illness and was abandoned by his friends. His body would be found three days later.

"He [Pliny the Elder] was in Miseno and, there, governed the fleet. It was just an hour after midday on August 24th when my mother pointed out to him a cloud that had just appeared of a size and shape that we had never seen before. [...] The cloud rose even higher and we did not know for sure which mountain it came from as we were looking on it from afar. It was only later that we discovered that the mountain was Mt. Vesuvius. Its shape was more like a pine tree than any other. As if starting from a huge trunk, the cloud swelled high into the sky, expanded and almost made branches. I believe that a vigorous blast of air, intact, pushed it upwards, then diminished or even abandoned it, or maybe even that its own weight overwhelmed it and the cloud soon formalized into a large umbrella shape. At times, it glittered immaculately white and at times it seemed dirty, streaked with markings according to the prevalence of ash or earth that it had raised into the air."

Pliny the Younger's first letter

4. Domenico Fontana's cover-up of Pompeii

The story of the great architect Domenico Fontana at Pompeii is really bizarre.

In the years between 1594 and 1600, the architect, already famous for grandiose works in Rome including the huge Egyptian obelisk in St. Peter's Square, accepted the much more humble project of laying out the water supply network for Naples, at the service of the Spanish Viceroy. Part of the project included the construction of a drainage channel in the Sarno valley, near what had been the city of Pompeii before its centuries-old destruction. During the work, the architect Fontana came across some brick buildings and saw fragments of a mosaic and impressions of human shapes appear in the walls beneath tons of earth.

The architect, however, after seeing these refined testimonies of an ancient past, ordered them to be covered up. We do not know whether Fontana suspected that there was the presence of an intact city under his feet or whether he was merely a pragmatic man, worried about meeting the deadlines for finishing his project. Those ruins, the first evidence found of the great civilization of Pompeii, would remain hidden for another 150 years. Oh ... if you want to see them, a stretch of the canal excavated by Domenico Fontana still blocks the path of tourists along Nocera Street, about 500 meters from the gate with the same name.

NEGLI ANNI 1594-1600 L'ARCHITETTO DOMENICO FONTANA SCAVÒ QUESTO CANALE PER PORTARE LE ACQUE DEL FIUME SARNO ALLE FABBRICHE D'ARMI DI TORRE ANNUNZIATA. DURANTE LA SUA COSTRUZIONE APPARVERO, PER LA PRIMA VOLTA, LE ROVINE DI POMPEI.

5. Strange coincidences at Pompeii: August 24th

A series of strange coincidences shows that August 24th is a really unlucky date for Pompeii!

August 24, 79 AD was the day of the terrible eruption, as evidenced in a letter from Pliny the Younger, reported as *"ante diem nonum kalendas septembres"*, that is, nine days before the calends of September (the first of the month), which corresponds exactly to August 24th. Ironically, just the day before, August 23rd, Pompeii had celebrated *Vulcanalia*, a celebration to appease the god Vulcano, which consisted of throwing small fish into a large communal fire as a symbolic replacement of their own lives. August 24, 1943, was also the day when a violent Anglo-American aerial bombardment fell on Pompeii based on reports of the presence of an inexistent German armored division entrenched within the archaeological area. The bombings caused considerable damage to many buildings especially in the southwest area of the city, where part of the Forum, the Porta Marina area and also the Pompeian museum (the Antiquarium) were hit, the latter struck by a powerful grenade that caused serious damage. A bomb also struck the house of the Superintendent, Amedeo Maiuri, who personally searched 5 hours in the rubble to retrieve notes, notebooks and books!!!

6. The earthquake of 62 AD: a "photo" of the time

Obviously at the time of the disastrous earthquake of 62 AD that had almost completely razed Pompeii to the ground, 17 years before the final

catastrophe, there were no cameras to document the damage done to buildings and structures in the city. The event is mentioned in ancient sources only because it occurred just as Emperor Nero was singing in a theater in Naples. There is, however, a marble frieze that, like a photograph, faithfully documents the state of Pompeii's public monuments after the earthquake. In the relief, which decorated the small sanctuary of the household gods at the house of *Caecilius Jucundus* (V 1, 23-25), depicted from left to right, the Forum of Pompeii with its honorary arch and the Temple of Jupiter can be seen having collapsed as a result of the earthquake. On the side of the staircase leading up to the main temple of the city, there are two large statues of gods on horseback with their bases embossed. On the right side of the relief, a group of Pompeiians gathered around an altar to make a sacrifice of atonement to the divinity of the earth (*Tellus*) to appease him after the earthquake. Another similar frieze depicted at *Castellum Aquae*, a large water reservoir located at the highest point of the city, shows Vesuvius Gate with its two doors open, a wagon drawn by a horse overturned by the force of the earthquake and a stretch of the adjoining wall with its masonry crumbling. But why did Caecilius Jucundus want to remember such a sad event in the shrine of his household gods? Perhaps, after personally witnessing these collapses and miraculously escaping the catastrophe, he wanted to offer an *ex voto* (a votive offering) to the protective gods for their protection.

7. Who were the victims of the eruption that destroyed Pompeii?

The question is always asked by visitors to the excavations, driven by the curiosity of seeing the expressions on the faces, the folds of the clothes, and

the twisted positions of the bodies in which the Pompeiians were surprised by the fury of Mt. Vesuvius. It is a tragedy that fascinates and humanizes the plaster casts of the bodies of the men, women and children who died there almost 2000 years ago. The entire family buried by the collapse of the basement of the House of the Golden Bracelet; the master and the slave at the door of the Villa of Diomedes who were trying to escape to the sea with the household treasure; the *paterfamilias* and his daughters in the Alley of the Skeletons holding the family's most valu- able goods, some jewels and the keys to the house; the Pompeiian who, daring to rob the homes that had been abandoned, found death at dawn on August 25th in the salesroom of a *Caupona* (tavern); the dog who was not able to break the chain that kept him tied to the House of Orpheus (VI 14, 18-20). These casts, a little over a hundred in number, were first made in 1863 by the director of the excavations at the time, Giuseppe Fiorelli. Having realized that there was a cavity left behind by the progressive decomposition of the body in the ash, he had it filled with

liquid plaster, recreating the shapes of the voids. The Fiorelli method also allowed excavators to restore the shapes of doors (you can see one at the entrance of the house of *Octavius Quartio* II 2 1-3), cabinets (go to the house of Julius Polybius) and, if applied on the ground, plant roots (like the casts of plane trees at the Large *Palaestra*). Today, this technique, combined with the wax casting of bronze statuary, has led to the creation of a plaster made of a transparent fiberglass material which can also restore the shape of any objects that are stuck to the body. In the resin cast of a young girl from Oplontis, found in a villa along with thirty-three other skeletons, almost all women and children, it is even possible to see the bracelet that the girl wore on her arm while trying to escape the catastrophe.

8. Lover's gossip on the walls of Pompeii

The entire city is full of inscriptions: electoral propaganda, an innkeeper's tab made in haste, words of love

written for a sweetheart, and support for gladiators are written in graffiti on the walls along the streets of Pompeii. It is a city both magical and mysterious for its sense of life and for showing us how it died, stopped suddenly at a moment that could have been from any day in time. On the very roads that are now woven together, stories of love and intrigue came to an end. A betrayed husband went out looking for witnesses to surprise his wife in flagrant adultery and stopped on the street, leaving a warning: *"We've got them! Romula is here with that lowlife!"* Soldiers and gladiators left graffiti on the walls with rough words of admiration for amorous exploits: *"Floronius, soldier of the 7th Legion, was here; few women knew of him and only six came to know him"*; *"Crescens, the retiarius, a gentleman to the ladies of the night,* *the morning and to others a doctor..."* A lover wrote a message to their beloved, adding a poetic phrase: *"Let the ones in love be in good health, let those who do not know how to love die, and let those who interfere in the natural course of love die twice."* Two gentle souls marked the scene of their first meeting: *"Romula and Staphylus met here"*, but a more clever response teased them: *"Here Staphylus met with Quieta." "A fair haired girl taught me to hate brunettes"* wrote a wounded lover, and another hand adds spontaneously: *"We hate them, but are happy to return!"* The living city of Pompeii and its inhabitants were so thirsty for that life that the walls describe so fully that some, exasperated, wrote in the margin of another person's graffiti: *"It is incredible, oh wall, that you have not yet fallen under the weight of so much nonsense"*.

C.I.L. IV 2487
ADMIROR TE PARIES NON CECIDISSE
QVI TOT SCRIPTORVM TAEDIA SVSTINEAS

9. The Amphitheater of Pompeii: were there really fights between men and beasts?

Looking at the Amphitheater of Pompeii, one of the oldest ever built, we are immediately reminded of the bloody scenes that we are accustomed

to seeing in movies set in ancient Rome: the hunts *(venationes)* in which armed men faced tigers, panthers, lions, bears, and bulls. You can almost see the 20,000 spectators sitting in the stands at the Pompeiian amphitheater, thirsty for blood and cheering on their favorites. In the *ima cavea* (the lowest section of seating), where guests had the best view, the magistrates in their white robes would have been seated. The multi-colored, disorderly working class would have sat in the *media cavea*. In the *summa cavea*, about 5 m higher than the arena, would have sat the women. The reality of these fights is far more complex and multifaceted than as seen in the movies and the idea in our imagination of men being consistently given to beasts as meals surely needs to be reconsidered. All evidence points to the fact that there were

never actually any wild beasts in the Amphitheater of Pompeii and that the prevailing fights were among the gladiators, man vs. man. Inscriptions painted on the walls announce the games, but make no mention of animals, nor does the Amphitheater seem to have had the technical arrangements necessary for the exhibition of large felines. The protective railing that separated the arena from the steps was painted with fight scenes between gladiators and is only 2.18 m high, too short to be have been able to contain leaping beasts! As well, unlike other similar buildings of the time, the arena does not have an underground area containing cages. It is therefore likely that in Pompeiian *venationes*, only animals of local fauna were exhibited, which were not able to jump or leap and give rise to unpleasant 'unscheduled' events. If we also consider that the recruitment of wild beasts was very expensive, as it would have meant taking a trip to Africa, their capture, their transport on special ships and their arrival at the destination, it may have been possible for these events to have occurred in Rome, but not in every small city in the Empire!

10. Pompeii during an election campaign

"I beg you to nominate G. Julius Polybius as the aedilis (magistratus). He brings good bread." "The fruit *growers ask for M. Ennius*

Sabinus as aedilis" "G. Julius Polybus, aedilis to take care of the roads, as well as the sacred and public buildings. Lantern maker, hold the ladder!" These proclamations would have been found in the time leading up to the vote, painted by special *dealbatores* in black or red on the walls of buildings along the busiest streets of Pompeii, just as today election posters are pasted all over cities during election campaigns. When the electoral process was set in motion, the city must have looked like a hive, with public speakers who held assemblies in the square and everyone discussing the programs and promises of the candidate in the streets, at the *thermopolium*, and at the baths! The notices were written by private citizens, neighborhood associates or craft corporations who did everything to present their candidates in a favorable light. They were often written at night and by people that were not exactly well-educated, as can be shown by the cursing mentioned above and transcribed at the end of the message in favor of Julius Polybius, referring to a not very steady lantern maker! *"Come on neighbors, do what you have to do!"* says one of the writings encouraging the electoral constituency of a district.

The formula was generally abbreviated with 3 initials *"O.V.F. Oro Vos Faciatis, please vote for"* and the name of the candidate being recommended. Everything good that could be said about the candidate was used: that he was a good and worthy man, clean, honest, virtuous, excellent, generous, and one who would never have spent public money. Messages in favor of a baker said, *"He will make good bread"*, another interesting slogan suggests *"Elect the one who got you elected"*, and another *"Those who strike through the messages are envious, hoping that you will get ill"*. Another seems very eloquent: *"How many lies are made for someone's ambition?"*. The lack of an electoral program demonstrates how the quality most appreciated by the community was the actual authority of the individual. Fruit growers, goldsmiths, and dyers mani-

fested their desire to have magistrates who promised prosperity for the city or for their social class. Although Pompeii was a Roman colony, it was given a large amount of administrative autonomy and the people could elect annually the *duoviri*, the highest authority of the colony with executive and partly judicial powers, and two *aedilis* responsible for the markets, festivals, shows and public order. At the end of the vote, festivals of thanksgiving were held in homes, streets, theaters, and some people even wrote about their satisfaction on the walls: *"The Pompeiians have unanimously elected Paquius Proculus as a duoviro: he is truly worthy of the town administration."* And the baker Proculus must have been a great person as no other Pompeiian citizen, and they were certainly not shy to speak, ever complained about him!!!

11. Clashes between Pompeiian and Nucerian Fans

"During that time, there was a fierce massacre between the Nucerians and Pompeiians, started for a worthless cause

on the occasion of the gladiatorial games announced by Livinieius Regulus, who as already mentioned, had been expelled from the Senate. From the beginning, they exchanged insults with the insolence of provincials, then passed to throwing stones, eventually resorting to arms, mostly in the hands of the citizens of Pompeii where the games were being held. Therefore, many of the Nucerians were taken home with wounds and many citizens from that city lamented the death of their children and their parents." This is the terrible report made by a historian of the time, Tacitus, of the clamorous violent event that broke out in 59 AD in the Amphitheater of Pompeii during a gladiator show between the fans of Pompeii and the guests from nearby *Nuceria Alfaterna*. In the stands of the great build-

ing, a tremendous brawl burst out which saw the Nucerians get the worst of it, literally massacred in the stands and any remaining survivors thrown out by the crowd. Emperor Nero brought the story before the Senate and the decision was made to close the Pompeiian amphitheater for 10 years, and Senator *Livineius Regulus*, the game organizer, and the other inciters of the riot were exiled. The report of this event is in same ways worrying as it reminds us of how little times have changed. Even today, whenever there is an event, there are always scalpers, peddlers, and Ultra fans with their cat-calls and slogans, unfortunately bringing violent outbursts, which is not really very sportsmanlike. The terrible fact of blood having being shed made a mark on public opinion, as

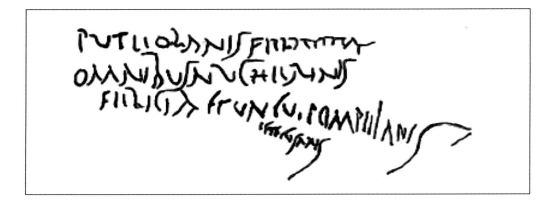

evidenced by a fresco found in a house in Pompeii that depicts that clash, as well as in graffiti found inside the House of the Dioscuri, referring to the incident: *"Campanians, you died along with the Nucerians in that victory!"* The stadium's ban was later downgraded to only two years, probably thanks to the requests of Poppea, the beloved wife of Nero, who apparently owned a villa in the regions around Pompeii.

12. A Pompeiian banker: *Lucius Caecilius Jucundus*

Even at Pompeii, there was what we would today call a "banker", someone who acted

as an intermediary in commercial transactions, was the lender for loans, and the agent in trading activities. We know the name of one of them: *Lucius Caecilius Jucundus*, who lived in a beautiful house near Porta Vesuvio (V I, 23). On the first floor of the house, there were large boxes containing tablets with registered contracts from many people living in the city. The 154 tablets that make up the banker's private archive, called "cerate" for the wax coating that was used to scratch out the text with a special pointed tool, were written between 52 and 62 AD, the year of the first earthquake that shook Pompeii. We do not know what happened to *Caecilius Jucundus'* office after that date: perhaps the massive damage caused by the earthquake caused him to take up a new occupation? Or did he choose to move away from the city center? Various types of contracts are registered on the tablets, many relating to loans, others to rentals or deposits, and still others to financial broking, for which the retained commission varies from 1 to 4%. *Caecilius Jucundus* organized auctions in which produce or industrial products were sold, acting as a guarantor of the payment and often fronting the money to the seller. In this way, the banker became the lender to the same

buyer, as in the contract with *Umbricia Ianuaria*, on behalf of whom he sells goods (of an unspecified type) equal to a sum of 11,039 sesterces (corresponding to approximately 20,000 Euros!) Here are some examples of the price ratio of goods commonly used at the time: 6.5 kg of wheat, 3 sesterces; a lit- tle more than ¼ liter of oil, 1 sesterce; 1 common measurement of wine, 1 as; 1 cup of Falerno wine, 1 sesterce. 520 sesterces were needed to buy a mule, for a silver cup, 360, for a tunic, 15, while for washing it, only 4 were needed, and the price of a slave was between 10,000 and 15,000 sesterces.

11,039 sesterces, which were given to L. Caecilius Jucundus following the auction (of the goods) of Umbricia Ianuaria. Excluding the fees (of Jucundus), the amount was paid, in agreement with Umbricia Ianuaria, by L. Caecilius Jucundus. Signed in Pompeii on December 12th.

Tablet 25, a contract with *Umbricia Ianuaria* from the archive of *Caecilius Jucundus*.

13. A clever entrepreneur: the perfumer of Pompeii

Roses, lilies, violets, basil and myrtle leaves, resins, roots, and aromatic seeds mixed with extra-virgin olive oil

obtained from squeezing green olives were the basic ingredients of perfumes from 2000 years ago that were manufactured in the perfumery shop in Pompeii. This clever resident had the ingenuity to set up the large garden of his own home (about 4000 m²) for the cultivation of olives and vines, but also of flowers, herbs and essences needed in the manufacturing of perfumes. In a huge tank full of oil purified of fat elements, he left flowers and leaves to soak, to which he could later add expensive oriental spices such as dill. Using various purification steps and after adding alcohol as the final step to purify the essences, the perfume was ready! The fragrances were kept in small glass or terracotta jars *(unguentaria)* or in precious alabaster boxes *(alabastra)* found almost everywhere throughout the house! The entrepreneur had ridden the wave of success, and considering that scents, fragrances, and creams were highly sought after by the matrons of the time, as well as by men, profits were really high. At the threshold of the house, a mosaic made of white tiles warned some customers: *"cras credo"*, *"I'll give you credit tomorrow"*. In the *triclinium*, the large dining room outside the house, near the

irrigation and seedling channels for tree planting, in an area filled with a sensual atmosphere, the perfumer gathered his friends at a banquet to celebrate business going well and to offer Hercules, whose statue can be found at the household altar placed on one side of the garden, a tithing of the earnings, as per Roman custom. You can visit this house (also called the Garden of Hercules II 8, 6) found along Nocera Street, and it is well worth seeing the seasonal blooms!

14. Let's have lunch at the *thermopolium* of *Lucius Vetutius Placidus!*

Just like in modern times, in Pompeii, it was common to consume the *prandium* (the mid-morning breakfast at

noon) outside the house, maybe even as a quick snack before going back to work or having a quick chat with a good friend. These "snack-bars" from 2000 years ago were called *thermopolia* and they were widespread throughout the city (89 in total). They were probably all like that of *Lucius Vetutius Placidus* along Via dell'Abbondanza (Regio I, Insula 8),

really full at peak times … On the large countertops with the characteristic L-shaped form, you can still find the *dolia* (terracotta containers) that contained the drinks and hot foods to be consumed on the spot. On the counter, covered in *opus sectile* (colorful marble segments that make geometric shapes), there was often a boiler to warm up ready-made dishes. *Lucius Vetutius Placidus*, the owner of the shop and the adjacent house, even left the proceeds of that unlucky day in 79 AD, hoping to come back and retrieve it at a later time. The contents of the money box are made up of small coins: 374 asses and 1,237 quadrants, for a total value of about 170 sesterces. On the wall, to the right of the counter, a *lara-rium* (sacred niche) with the depiction of the Lares and the Genius of the master was placed to propitiate the good fortune of the house, while the protection of the "shop" would have been entrusted to the protective deities of commerce and wine, Mercury and Dionysus, painted on both sides of the niche. But *Lucius Vetutius Placidus' thermopolium* was not just a snack-bar, as it had one or more back rooms where patrons could sit down to eat comfortably lying on *triclinii*. And in the summer season, which in the shadow of Vesuvius lasted at least 7 months, a meal could be eaten in an indoor garden with an open air *triclinium*, shaded by vineyards and flowerbeds planted with aromatic plants.

15. Profane love at Pompeii...

"Hic habitat felicitas", happiness dwells here, recites the sign accompanying the representation of a phallus at

the entrance to a building in Pompeii. The city, under the protection of the goddess Venus, was in fact a happy city, dedicated to love in all its forms, even the paid-for type! That is why Pompeii would not have been complete without a brothel, the Lupanar, the "lupa (she-wolf)" which in Latin meant prostitute. It was a small 2-storey building, not far from the crowded Stabian Baths. Here,

a plate of uneaten pasta and beans was found, perhaps left behind by a customer hurrying to escape some bad guys! On the ground floor, there were 5 small narrow rooms (*cellae meretriciae*) closed by wooden doors, almost entirely occupied by masonry beds (which we hope had mattresses on them!). What always attracts the curious looks of tourists are the paintings on the outside

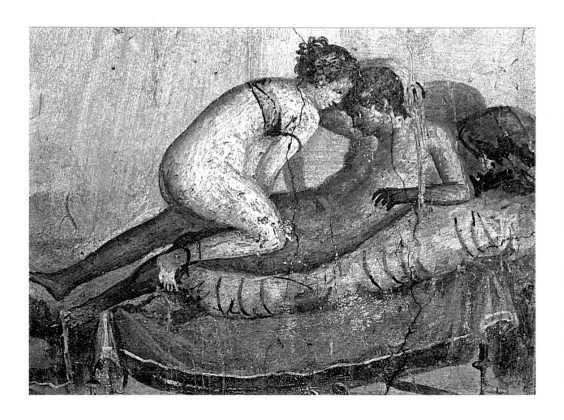

of each room, depicting couples in different erotic positions! It was not an unusual scene in Pompeii, where even at the Suburban Baths, many workshops or even bedrooms in houses contained erotic paintings. Sexuality in Roman society, free from the thought of sin, was an integral part of man's earthly dimension. The construction of the Lupanar dates back to the final days of the city, as evidenced by the imprint of a coin from 72 AD preserved in the fresh plaster of a room. But that does not mean that there would not have been such a place in the years before: in taverns and inns, sexual activity could be carried out sporadically or peripherally in the baths, or even in single rooms with doors that opened directly onto the street. From writing in graffiti on the walls of Pompeii, for example, we know that at the House of the Vettii, *Eutychides* carried out his business and was known to be Greek and to have gentle manners. The price of prostitutes, generally Greek or Eastern, was inexpensive and ranged from 2 to 8 asses (a good cup of wine cost 1), but there were also cheaper ones: *"sum tua aere"*, "I'm yours for a copper" wrote one anonymous prostitute near the entrance of their home.

16. After work... let's all go to the baths!

Just as people today go to the gym, after a long day of intense work, the Pompeiians headed

to the baths. They went to public baths, not only to care for their bodies, but also to meet friends, chat, do business or discuss political affairs. In Pompeii, there was plenty of choice where to go: 3 bath buildings were located at the intersection of the most important road junctions: the Stabian Baths, the oldest; the Baths of the Forum, built around 80 BC, and the newest baths, the Central Baths, which were started after the earthquake of 62 AD and still under construction at the time of the erup-

tion. After leaving their clothes in the dressing room (*apodyterium*), Pompeiians, with linen or woolen towels, could go for a swim in the outdoor pool (*natatio*), exercise in the outdoor gym or play games: track for adults and ball for younger clients. Then came time for the baths, enjoyed in order according to the temperature of the water. In the warm bath room, the *calidarium*, the temperature could reach up to 60 degrees, but cold water in the basin (*labrum*) gave bathers some cool refreshment. We even

know the cost of the *labrum* from the Baths of the Forum which had been donated by the city *duoviri*: 5240 sesterces! After a break in the moderately heated space of the *tepidarium*, Pompeiians toughened themselves up in the cool waters of the *frigidarium*. The more modern Central Baths were also equipped with *laconicum*, a kind of sauna with very hot dry air obtained from a hot air flow moving under the raised floor and through passages in the walls. After the bath, patrons were massaged to activate their blood circulation or to better clean their skin using perfumed ointments. Both men and women went to the baths, but in separate sections; entrance was usually after 1:30 pm and the baths stayed open until late in the evenings as is attested by the numerous oil lamps that were found that would have illuminated the areas of the baths at night. Bathers would have paid a small fee at the entrance and kids were free, although there were different prices for the various services: safekeeping of clothing, massages, providing perfumed oils… A motto written on one of the walls of Pompeii explains the baths perfectly: "*Baths, wine, and love weaken our bodies, but they are the substance of life.*"

17. Gladiators at Pompeii: *morituri te salutant?* (We, who are about to die, salute you?)

Red paintings on the walls of Pompeii, the ancestors of modern billboards, announced the gladiatorial games.

Gladiators took to the arena accompanied by their finest polished weapons, while the audience, excited, screamed the names of their favorites. They stood in a row in front of the organizer's stage and greeted the crowd two at a time with the traditional ritual formula *"morituri te salutant"*, that is, "we, who are about to die, salute you". They were then separated into pairs of fighters and a referee who, like in modern fighting rings, checked that the weapons being used met regulations. Having been assured of this, he traced a circle in the middle of the arena where the fight would take place. After a nod, the fight began with skillful moves on both sides, the orchestra beating their instruments, and the public shouting enthusiastically: the uproar was tremendous! A gladiator fell wounded, unable to de-

fend themselves: the audience shouted out *"iugula"* (slit their throat) or *"mitte"* (let them live). If the verdict of the crowd was unfavorable for the defeated gladiator, the winner traditionally slit the throat of their opponent and then took a tour of the arena holding a palm frond, urged on by the standing ovation of the public. In spite of this scene which we are accustomed to seeing in so many cinematic performances, the announcements of the performances painted along the streets of Pompeii (*edicta munerum*) and the graffiti written by both gladiators and their *fans* provide us with a different picture of the outcome of gladiatorial games. Beside the picture of each gladiator is marked their name, total number of fights in their career and an acronym, which refers to the outcome of the last fight, the

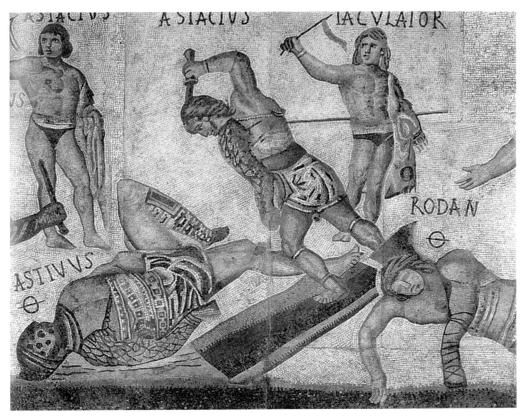

one at which the graffiti writer was apparently present. The letter 'V' indicated that the gladiator had won (*vicit*); 'M' stood for *missus*, the gladiator had lost the fight but had been pardoned; the letter 'P' stood for *perit*, and the gladiator was dead. Out of a total of 32 fights, only 5 gladiators had died: it was obviously in everyone's best interest to not let a professional gladiator die whose training had cost time and money. In almost all of the fights, the defeated gladiator was pardoned. Even the number of fights that each gladiator fought confirms this: they sometimes exceeded 70 fights!

18. Pink Floyd: *Live at Pompeii*

Pompeii has been the backdrop for numerous stories set purposefully among the monuments and houses of the city.

Images of Pompeii can be seen in countless theatrical, circus and cinematic stage scenery. Even the fact that the legendary band Pink Floyd chose Pompeii to shoot a video may not be known by everyone! In 1972, Pink Floyd, by then already famous, performed a concert at the Amphitheater of Pompeii without any public spectators, with only the presence of the technical staff. From the recording, the director Adrian Maben created a live-film concert, *Live at Pompeii*, which is even today a milestone in rock history for the audio-visual effects used in an empty space. The idea of making a film in Pompeii came to the director during a day of sightseeing in the city: Maben realized that he had lost his wallet and convinced that he had left it at the Amphitheater, returned there in the evening to look for it. He was so enchanted by the magical and mysterious atmosphere of the Amphitheater in the dark that he said, *"Pink Floyd must come here!"* The film, co-produced with French television, is also the source of a series of anecdotes, the most well-known being about the supply of electrical current needed for the band and stage projectors. Since there was not enough power in the archaeological area, producers had to hurriedly

extend an electrical line a few kilometers to Pompeii, "planted" in the fields, day and night, by numerous volunteers, in order to avoid damage or breaks in the line due to any unauthorized attachments. Due to this inconvenience, the six-day shooting time was reduced to three and, as there was not enough footage to record all the necessary material, the director was forced to use studio-played portions to which a background was later applied. In addition, to further aggravate the situation, a delayed flight coming from London caused the instrument cases to be delivered late, leaving Pink Floyd only two days to shoot the entire movie!

19. *Mensa Ponderaria* and Public Washrooms in the Forum of Pompeii: signs of civilization!!!

Imagine being a merchant coming to Pompeii 2000 years ago after a long tiring journey

by wagon (*plaustrum*) to carry your goods to the city. You enter Porta Marina, stop for a quick moment at the Temple of Apollo to thank the god for having successfully made the trip and then immediately enter the Civic Forum of the city, contributing to its daily noises and smells. The atmosphere of the main square of Pompeii, the center of religious, political and commercial life, resembled that of Arabic *medinas* or *souqs* complete with the romantic backdrop of Jupiter's temple that we are accustomed to seeing! The holler of the town crier, the prices of the products on sale in the workshops and food shops being called out to customers, the bustle of the people waiting outside the basilica, the echo of the blacksmith's strikes, the screeching of the grinding mills, the sounds of animals, the squeak of wagons, the shouting of the mob ... In all this chaos, think how easy it would

have been for an unlucky trader to come across unruly swindlers! For this exact reason, in order to restrict sellers' liberty, the town council set up an office in the Forum displaying a table with the legal weight and capacity measurements, called a *mensa ponderaria* (measuring table). On the large limestone table, there were nine circular depressions, each corresponding to one measurement. A hole in the bottom of each allowed the weighed merchandise to pour out. In the interests of efficiency, after the colony of Pompeii was founded and the measurements of the Osci were abandoned, the depressions in the table were adapted to the new units from the Roman system even if they did not match the previous ones! Right beside the Forum of Pompeii, merchants could safely take care of their physical needs in a free public washroom (*forica*), consisting of a large room with a seat covered by perforated boards capable of simultaneously accommodating more than ten people!

20. The *lanista* of Pompeii

Brought to international fame a few years ago by the film starring Russell Crowe, the figure of the gladiator has always aroused

great interest in spectators. But the fact that the gladiatorial games originated in Campania and that there was more than one gladiator school in Pompeii is not as well known... The school, run by a *lanista* who was the trainer and owner of the gladiators, was a mixture between a sports center and a barracks. In the house known as the *Sacerdos Amandus* (I 7,7), there lived a *lanista* who advertised his craft by means of a painting at the entrance depicting a fight scene between gladiators. The gladiators pictured were accompanied by their names: Spartacus is the most requested! Their training was very hard, considered similar to that of modern karate, and took place either in the Large *Palaestra* near the Amphitheater, or, in the latter period of the city, at the *Quadriporticus* of the Large Theater ... There was a code of

honor and a spirit of camaraderie that linked many of the gladiators, usually former slaves or ex-criminals freed by their own victories. Honor and courage: fleeing from the battle was not an option! Depending on the type of armor worn and the mode of fighting, gladiators were divided into very precise groups that fought each other. The *thraex* gladiators carried the *sica*, a characteristic short, curved sword bent at right angles and had a small, round shield for defense. Their body was protected by armor, two greaves and a metal arm protector. A visor covered their entire face. The sworn enemies of the *thraeces* were the *hoplomachi* with their imposing helmets decorated with feathers. Their heavy armor and huge rectangular shield, behind which they retreated completely when being attacked, made them very

slow. Another traditional pairing was formed by the *retiarius* who used both a trident and a net at the same time to keep away the *secutors*, their usual opponents, and block their attacks. *Secutors*, avoiding the *retiarius'* weapons behind the protection of a rectangular shield, confronted the *retiarius* with the *gladio*, the typical Roman short, straight sword. They wore small, rounded helmets to not allow any chance for an opponent to grab onto it. Other groups of gladiators included the *essedarii* that fought on wagons dressed like Britons and *bestiari* that fought against animals. The private organizer of the games "rented" the gladiators from the *lanista*: if a gladiator returned mortally wounded or dead, the price was considerably higher! But since the show was usually a form of electoral propaganda, letting gladiators be killed in the arena became a way for those who sponsored the games to demonstrate their generosity ... the price did not matter as long as the public thirst for blood was satisfied!

21. "Pleasure baths" at Pompeii

Unscrupulous entrepreneurs existed even 2000 years ago in Pompeii! This is the case of the owner of the

Suburban Baths, who had the idea of trying to entice the largest number of customers to his establishment through the use of sexual advertising, more or less similar to what can be seen today in many examples of communication by the media. The entrepreneur constructed the Suburban Baths outside the walls of Pompeii near the entrance to Porta Marina, in an area close to the river and the busy harbor of the city. The establishment was conceived differently from previous Pompeiian thermal buildings, without a division of sectors and with a single dressing room for both men and women. To the usual sequence of bathing rooms at different temperatures and a room for sweat baths, another room equipped with a large heated pool with the samovar system (a container placed in the center which contained a fire) was added. Sex as a promotional item was used in the dressing room decorations, where erotic scenes were combined with numbers and compartments where customers placed their clothes before starting the bathing sequence. The frescoes showed various sexual positions and performances and formed a sort of "catalog" of the illicit activities that took place on the upper floors. It is not by chance that the Romans combined the ideas of love and baths according to the saying: *"balnea vina venus corrumpunt corpora nostra sed vitam faciunt"* "baths, wine and love corrupt our bodies, but they make life beautiful". Among the peculiarities that can be found aside from the image of a naked poet, there is also the scene of love between two women, the only scene of lesbian love that has come to us from the Roman era.

22. The Large Theatre

Did you know that the theater of Pompeii is one of the oldest in the Roman world and that it was built 150 years

before those in Rome? Although they preferred the rougher performances of the Amphitheater, Pompeiians did not turn their noses at theatrical performances, even though the tendency of offering performances during religious festivals led to them becoming rare events and creating a long waiting list in the city! As in some places today, going to the theater was an opportunity not only to "see", but to "be seen": from fancy clothes, to comfortable, luxurious seats made for two people (*bisellia*) on which aristocrats took their place in the front rows. Tragedies and comedies were offered at the same time, following an intentional mix of the genres also attested to by the frescoes of the Centenary House, where tragic scenes were painted alongside comic ones. One of

the more successful authors of comedies was the Athenian Menander, whose portrait showed him with a head crowned by the peristyle of a house not far from the theater; the Roman playwright Plautus was also much loved. The "playbill" was painted on the walls of the streets a few days before the show, or called out in the Forum by heralds paid by the show organizers, usually the magistrates in office. It was up to them to fund the shows, and indeed, show generosity, as theatrical performances were an essential requirement of aspiring to future public office! The charm of theatrical performances was not only to be found in the skill of the actors, but also in the painted sets, along with the presence of special technology that produced effects that captivated the

audience. Since entrance was free and the performances were of prolonged duration, there was no lack of people to occupy the seats some arriving to get a place even the night before! The theater was in the open air (at the most, a *velarium* protected spectators from the sun), but in the event of severe, sudden bad weather, spectators could take refuge under the porches of the large courtyard behind the backdrop, where many street vendors offered refreshments. What else? Oh, yes, the theater of Pompeii boasted a curtain, but it operated in the exact opposite way of a modern one, being lowered at the beginning and raised at the end of the show!

23. Sator Square: were there Christians at Pompeii?

As is well-known, the eruption of Mt. Vesuvius interrupted life in Pompeii in 79 AD. That means that only 46 years had passed since the death of Christ

in 33 AD, and that the first followers of the Christian religion, born at the periphery of the Empire, had not been practicing for very long. It is curious, therefore, to find concrete evidence of Christian presence in a town like Pompeii, far from Palestine and certainly not made up of the cosmopolitan culture that characterized Rome! Yet in Pompeii, graffiti have been found referring to a Christian matrix, seen in the case of the famous *Pater Noster* cryptogram, also known as a Sator square, written in graffiti in a room of the House of *Paquius Proculus* (I 7, 1-20) and also on a column of the Large *Palaestra*. Many theories have been put forth for the meaning of this Sator square, of which Pompeii's example is the oldest attestation, ranging from pre-Christian symbols to encrypted messages from the Templars. It is made up of a series of five words each with five letters (*sator arepo tenet opera rotas*), written one below another so as to form a square which can be read in any direction. The 25 letters, broken down and re-composed, form the expression *Pater Noster* twice. If you read the square in a zigzag direction, the expression "*sator opera tenet – tenet opera sator*" can also be found, that is, "the sower possessed the art",

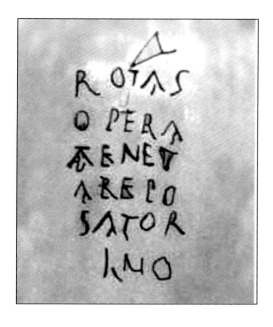

that is, the master of creation. And yet, the intersection of the two words *tenet* draws a perfect cross in the center of the square: it could have been an encrypted representation made by early Christians in order to worship the cross in secret. Sator squares remain a mystery, though the hypothesis of a Christian presence in Pompeii would not be without foundation and could be connected to the existence of Jewish groups in the valley of the Sarno, who would have been the first to be able to recognize the Christian message.

24. Pompeii: «Vine Leaves are back, Human Life is back!»

This motto encompasses the initiative promoted by Pompeii's Archaeological Park which in 1996

began the "Villa dei Misteri" project, with the objective of restoring the viti-culture of the area using the same vines that would have been found at the time of the eruption. Three of the eight types cultivated in ancient Pompeii were re-planted, producing the highly sought after *Vesuvinum*, which saw amphorae exported to Spain, Gaul and Britain. The blend was made up of aglianico, sciascinoso and piedirosso grapes.

Pompeiians knew how to produce this wine, having learned the secret through years of experimentation and cultivation. They primarily used the *"Murgentina"* vine, which came from the Sicilian city of Morgantina, and at Pompeii had such great success that they changed its name to *"Pompeiana"*, but also the *Holconia* vine, originally from Etruria. Wine-making facilities (*torcularia*) were found in many villas in the area of Mt. Vesuvius containing presses for squeezing grapes with ram-headed trunks and large semi-finished terracotta amphorae for storing wine ... At that time, wine was said to have had the gelatinous texture of jam and had to be diluted with water ... The *Arrii* were wine producers at Pompeii; they produced *Asinio Proculo* wine, known for a particular characteristic, *Asiniano racemato*, a sort of D.O.C. of the era. The *Vettii, Conviva* and *Restituto* brothers were also famous, having gotten rich from making wine and selling it at large events and then building the wonderful home where they lived. *Eusino* the innkeeper was well-known in Pompeii, it was enough to write "for Eusino" on the amphorae that were intended for him, and the product would reach him even in the cellars. The vineyards were replanted according to ancient methods: rows were placed close together follow-ing the imprints left 2000 years ago, identified by plaster casts of the roots, and were about 4 feet apart (each foot measured 29.64 cm) and supported by chestnut wood pallets according to the system of *"vitis compluviata"* de-scribed in the "Natural History" writ-ten by the same Pliny the Elder that fell victim to the eruption! The 5 areas

of the vineyards are located in Regio I and II near the Amphitheater (the vineyards of the innkeeper Eusino, the House of the Ship Europa, the Osteria of the Gladiator, the Forum Boarium, and the House of the Faun) and cov-er an area of about one hectare! Two bottles of Pompeiian red Typical Geo-graphic Indication (IGT) were sent to Italian embassies all over the world to show them how Campania knew how to be *"felix* (happy)" even today!

25. Today, December 17th at Pompeii...

We are in Pompeii, it's cold, and it's December 17th. This day, which casually coincides

with my birthday (or rather *dies natalis* if we stay in context), is the date that marked the beginning of the Saturnalia festival throughout the Roman world. It was the most popular festival of all times, held in honor of the ancient god Saturn, founder of the mythical Golden Age. A feast of magical fantasy, where possibility took the place of necessity in history and where everyone, on this day, was obliged to wear the *pileus*, the conical felt hat usually reserved for freed slaves. Everything in the city stopped for a day:

schools and courts were closed, debates were suspended and executions against criminals were delayed. In homes, in front of the family's household shrine, an offering was made of an unweaned piglet, and candles were lit to symbolize the sun re-emerging after the winter when the days began to lengthen once more. At the feast, all members of the family were allowed to eat and drink as much as they wanted, to play dice, to joke, and they all followed a nominated king of revelry chosen in the most bizarre, unusual ways. Just like at a great carnival, the division between free men and slaves disappeared on this day and for once, the slaves got to sit at the master's table, not by concession, but as equals, to the point that they could tell them everything that they would not dare

to at any other moment. It is easy to imagine how on December 17th, all the *cauponae* (taverns) and *thermopolia* (snack bars) in the city would have been full: patrons drank wine, ate focaccia (without tomatoes, which had not yet been discovered), sausage accompanied by the not-to-be-missed *garum* (a fish sauce), onions (*cepæ*) and cabbage (*brassicæ*). Who knows how many customers there were at the *caupona* of Asellina (IX 11, 2), who personally managed her own tavern on Via dell'Abbondanza. There, patrons could enjoy a trendy cocktail, the *"posca"*, obtained by mixing water, eggs, and acidic wine. The venue was also known for another quality: the service that was provided by three attractive, accommodating Eastern girls: *Smiryna, Maria* and *Egle* ...

26. Isis: the crying goddess

Veneration for the goddess Isis, the bride, mother and protector of the sailors, in Pompeii and in the Roman world was very widespread.

But how did the worship of a foreign deity succeed in replacing traditional divinities in Pompeii? Isis was an unhappy Goddess who was persecuted by the envious god Seth who killed her beloved husband Osiris and forced her to hide with her son Harpocrates in the swamps of the Nile Delta, wandering in search of the dismembered body of her spouse. She was the goddess who wept for humanity, a heartfelt, sorrowful cry that gave life back to the earth because her tears replenished the waters of the Nile, which, when it flooded, fertilized the land of Egypt. Water was therefore

the dominant element in all ceremonies to honor her. The anniversary of Osiris's death, the painstaking search for body parts, and the joy of resurrection was re-enacted during the *Isia*, from November 13th to 16th, when the ritual calls for purification of the faithful with the sacred water of the Nile. Water was collected in a monumental bowl at the Temple of Isis at Pompeii and was used for the initiation of new worshippers to the cult. Every day, the statue of the goddess was washed and dressed; the water from the river was blessed by hymns from the priests, who, in turn, were completely shaved, and had to carry out ablutions themselves, both day and night. One of the priests of Isis, *D. Octavius Quartio*, built two perpendicular water channels (*euripi*) in the vast garden of his home in Pompeii decorated with statues and fountains related to Egypt, where artificially created floods simulated sacred ones in the fertile area of the Nile. This was Isis. We could also add that early Christian culture owes a great debt to the cult of Isis both in terms of rituals and iconography (the goddess is represented with her son in her arms), and various temples dedicated to her have been transformed into Marian churches! Indeed, devotion to Isis was not that dissimilar to the cult of the Blessed Virgin of the Rosary practiced in the very popular Sanctuary of Pompeii!

27. The jeweled matron and the gladiator

This is one of the urban legends that I heard in Pompeii and that I will now pass on to you. In ancient times, just like today,

myths about gladiators were alive and well amongst the people: they were some for gladiators who had become really famous among the spectators of the arena and were given unrestrained fanfare, and among the people who sought at all costs to become a gladiator, just as today people wish to become successful athletes. Pompeiian graffiti provides proof of the admiration that the gladiators enjoyed especially among the female members of the audience. We know of *Celadus the Thraex* "magnificent and longed for by the girls", of the *Retiarius Crescens* "master of the maidens", "doctor of the ladies of the night, the morning and all the others" ... It is also well-known that some gladiators became the lovers of rich matrons and widows: rumors existed that even Commodus was not the son of Emperor Marcus Aurelius, but rather of his mother's lover, a gladiator. Some of the finds from Pompeii may confirm that high-class ladies were particularly sensitive to the charm of gladiators ... In the 18th century, helmets, shin guards, shields, lances, and richly decorated daggers were found in the *Quadriporticus* of the Theater of Pompeii. These are all parts of the armor used in the parades that preceded the gladiatorial fights. In the last phase of the city's life, the *Quadriporticus* behind the backdrop of the theater was used as a barracks and gladiatorial accommodation, perhaps because the one normally used on Nola Street had been damaged by the earthquake in 62 AD. In the cells where they slept, in addition to personal belongings, the remains of a female adorned with a wealth of jewelry were also found. What was a rich, noble Pompeiian matron doing in the barracks? Exercising a bit of imagination perhaps, the idea that she could be free of entanglements for one night, presumably hidden, spending time with her beautiful gladiator. As a final note about this unfortunate affair of love and death, another body found near a horse was identified as the slave that had accompanied the rich matron. Who knows if the cataclysmic event surprised him just as he arrived or as he was about to go home? Whatever it was, we can assume he died at a happy moment.

28. A walk along Via dell'Abbondanza on a Saturday

Today is Saturday, market day in Pompeii. Zosimus, the potter, a highly appreciated manufacturer of sturdy jars for *garum*, noted on the wall of his workshop

located not far from the Amphitheater a list of the *nundinae* (regular market days) along with the days of periodic markets in the cities around Pompeii. The market in Nuceria was held on Sundays, in Nola on Tuesdays, in Cumae on Wednesdays, in Puteoli on Thursdays, in Capua on Fridays, and in Atella on Mondays. The Forum and the streets are full of people and Via dell'Abbondanza is an uninterrupted succession of workshops, shops, taverns and inns. There is the *taberna pomaria* of *Felix* (I 8, 1), the

fruit grower, who exhibits his products on the counter. A little further along can be found the corian workshop, the only tannery in the city. The 15 tanks where the skins were left to soak in water together with vegetable extracts would certainly not have been a delight for the nose!! Nor would a good smell have come from the neighboring shop owned by *Stephanus,* the *Fullonica* (Fullery I 6, 7) ! At the dry cleaners, fabrics, after having being pressed, were rinsed out in tanks with degreasing substances such as baking soda and human urine. And, to prove that *pecunia non olet* (money does not smell), jars were placed along the street for passersby who were always willing to donate a little. That was, of course, before Vespasian introduced taxes! The final proceeds taken in by the fullery speak plain: 1,089.50 sesterces, not bad, if you consider that the annual rent of a fullery was 1,652! At the *thermopolium* di *Vetutius Placidus* (I 8, 8), you can enjoy a cup of hot wine because today is Saturday. Earnings are good here, testified by the almost 3 kg of coins found in the container collected at the counter! A little further along, the unmistakable noise of a grinder can be heard coming from the *pistrinum* where bread was pro-

duced: the mills, manned by oxen or slaves, ground up the grain to make the flour for donuts that had an irresistible aroma! A shed protected the next two lodgings from the sun, the *caupona* (tavern) of *Sotericus* and the Insegna d'Africa (I 12, 3) where, besides the bean soup or the poor wine, the names of certain *puellae* (maidens) tempted adventurous patrons. And then there is the *garum* workshop of the *Umbricii*, an indispensable condiment used in Roman cuisine made by letting the interior of numerous varieties of fish ferment in the sun. The *garum* of Pompeii was renowned! This would also not be a recommended place for a wayfarer to stop for long...

29. Cave canem (Beware of the dog)!!!

(C)ave Canem, literally "beware of the dog" is still used today

at the entrance of houses to warn visitors of the presence of a guard dog. But did you know that the motto derives from the famous mosaic with the black dog on the leash (*canis catenarius*) accompanied by the inscription "*Cave Canem*" located on the floor of the entrance of the House of the Tragic Poet (VI 8, 3)? And that many other homes in Pompeii reproduced the image of a dog guarding the dwelling at night without the lights of Pompeii? A black dog, without an inscription, is depicted held by a chain at a semi-open door in a mosaic placed at the entrance of the House of *Paquius Proculus.* "A similar subject is painted also at the entrance of the House of Orpheus (VI 14, 20), and a dog without a chain is painted on a pillar at the entrance of the *Caupona* (tavern) of *Sotericus* (I 12, 3). A funny anecdote narrated by Petronius in his *Satyricon* mentions this habit: one of the 'nouveau richè, Trimalchio, painted a dog on the left wall of the entrance of the house that was so enormous that it even scared Petronius when he entered: *"I looked at it curiously, and jumped back so suddenly that I almost broke my leg. On the left, next to the doorman's station, was painted a large dog on a chain which looked real and had the caption "Cave Canem" written below it.* Proof was found that there were real guard dogs that actually guarded the *aditus* (opening) of Pompeiian homes in the form of a dog, now seen in a plaster casting, still tied at the collar to a chain at the House of Orpheus!

30. Priestess *Eumachia*

Pompeii was also home to some great women, *Aesquilia Polla*, who died at age 22,

whose husband, an important politician at the time of Augustus, erected just outside Porta Nola the most elegant tomb that was ever built for a beautiful young woman. Julia Felix, owner and attentive administrator of her large villa in the city. The priestess *Mamia*, who built the Temple of the Genius of Augustus in the Forum, and for whom the Senate decreed that a tomb be built outside Porta Ercolano with a view of Mt. Vesuvius that inspired Goethe's poetic verses. But the greatest of all was *Eumachia*, priestess of Venus and patron saint of the most powerful and numerous association in the city, the *Fullones*, the laundrywomen. Eumachia, a descendent of a family of entrepreneurs, was so rich that she built the large building located on the eastern side of the square of the Forum of Pompeii at her own expense, dedicating it to Livia, the Emperor's wife, and honoring her by placing a statue at the large open exedra within the porch! Eumachia's building, primarily intended for Imperial worship, was also the city's most important trading venue. Various types of transactions took place there: from the sale of clothes and wool to the slave trade to auctioneers' and bankers' auctions. A small room, outfitted with a large container used as a resonator pot, was used for announcements made by the herald! The fountain, next to the side entrance of the building and decorated with the image of a cornucopia, was the inspiration for the name Via dell'Abbondanza! Even the large exedra-shaped tomb in the necropolis of Porta Nocera necropolis is an important sign of how powerful Eumachia was. She also built the largest, most monumental sepulcher in Pompeii for herself and her family: from the highest floor of the monument, her statue reminded those who entered the city of how prestigious she had been. Her likeness must have been known throughout the city: even one of the buildings near the Forum contained an honorary statue dedicated to Eumachia by the *Fullones*!

31. Inside *Salvius' Caupona* (tavern): gambling in Pompeii

So great was the love of Pompeiians for gambling that every establishment had a hidden gaming room in the back and in spite of the ban by the

censors that restricted gambling to the days of *Saturnalia* only, the practice of "dice" games, which had become a real social problem because of the constant uproar it caused, continued daily as people were able to make bets and play dice in the city. There were two types, *tali* (knucklebones), which were oblong in shape and had only four numbered faces, and *tesserae* (dice) with six faces which were thrown out of a container (*fritillus*); the winner was the player who got the highest score. In some places, it was also possible to play *navia aut capita* (heads or crosses), *par impar* (even and odd), *micatio* (the modern game of Morra) or *tric trac*. What was it? An ancient version of snakes and ladders. A table was marked with twelve intersecting lines and game pieces moved according to the score obtained

by throwing the dice and knucklebones. One of the trendiest places for gambling enthusiasts was *Salvius' Caupona* (Tavern VI 14, 36) ... The warm wine that made patrons' heads spin was the house specialty; *Salvius* kept it in a heated container on a lead boiler placed over the fire. In the back of the tavern, patrons could also be entertained by available *puellae* (maidens) and throw some dice, but sometimes the disagreements between players ended up in violent mischief!! This is exactly what *Salvius* had painted in frescoes on the shop's walls: there were 4 scenes illustrated with cartoons of painted inscriptions. *Myrtale*, the prostitute, kissed a customer of the *Caupona* (tavern), while two other clients argued over the priority of their order with a hostess. A vicious argument had broken out between card players: *"I'm out"*, said the first, but the other replied *"But it was two, not three"*. Insults flew between them, *"You're a born fellator, it was I that won"* and they resorted to using their fists. But then the little innkeeper intervenes with a peremptory order: *"Take it outside."*

32. The last war of Pompeii

It was the spring of 89 BC and Pompeii had joined the cause of the Italian member-states fighting to win the right to Roman citizenship and as a result

became an enemy of Rome. It was not long before they felt the consequences of their actions. The commander of the Roman army, General *Lucius Cornelius Silla*, decided to attack the northern section of the city between Porta Ercolano and Porta Vesuvio. It was undoubtedly the strongest segment of the entire fortification wall, well-armed and defended by the three towers, but from the edge of the surrounding trench to the base of the volcano, there was a wide plain perfect for the deployment of heavy catapults and ballistae. As the armaments and tactics of both the besieged and the besiegers were Roman, it was clear from the outset that the city would not fall for a simple handshake, but only after a grueling siege. The preparations were meticulous and the war machines were loaded with ammunition until, at dawn on a clear summer day, the order to fire was given. The signal was heard even from the walls of Pompeii, where inhabitants were anxiously spying on the movements of the army. A few moments later, following some menacing screeches, a hail of stone balls crashed against the battlements, smashing them along with the defensive parapets. A host of arrows, penetrating the breaches

in the walls, struck many inhabitants paralyzed by the horror and violence of the scene, it was unforgettable. Armor and shields were worth nothing. A reddish stain slowly poured down from the terraces, and between the echo of blasts, the whistle of arrows, hiss of catapults and screams of the wounded could be heard even from the towers that were counterattacking with artillery. Pompeii defended itself whole-heartedly, and at first, the Romans were forced to fall back, but a short time later, they earned a victory over the Celts, Pompeii's allies near Nola in a battle in which approximately 18,000 men lost their lives. Inside the city, the effects of the siege were evident: houses were torn apart by strikes made over the walls, others were burned by incendiary projectiles that fell on the town at night ... Pompeii and its allies lost the war, Rome re-established sovereignty and the city, transformed into a Roman colony, recovered its state of well-being shortly afterwards, forgetting this tragic trial. But some citizens still remembered, preserving, maybe superstitiously, the stone balls that had fallen during the extravagant fratricidal battle that took place in their homes ...

33. The last baked goods from Modesto's bakery

Liberally taken from a excerpt written in 1955 by then Superintendent of Pompeii, Amedeo Maiuri, in

"Pompei ed Ercolano tra case ed abitanti". The house, with a bakery and a shop, was on Via Augustali, flanked on one side by the residence of the centurion *Caesius Blandus* showing off who knows how many trophies, and on the other side by that of the brothers *Sirico* and *Nummiano*, who were extremely rich, and who had placed an invitation for their most welcome guest on their entry threshold: *"Salve Lucrum"*, "Welcome profits!". The baker's name was Modesto, as announced on a painted electoral program right next to the entrance. Modesto had bought a noble house that had been destroyed by the earthquake in a neighborhood

of high-class citizens and turned it into a bakery, sacrificing the frescoes and mosaics. The animal stable replaced the foyer, the basin for rinsing grain took the place of the *impluvium* (watershed), and the workshop for kneading the dough was where the *triclinium* would have been, leaving the grinding mills and kiln where the *tablinum* and garden were before. He and his family lived in the areas remaining on the upper floor. Modesto was a hard-worker, even because only a few steps away, with his bakery open to passersby along Via Stabiana was the king of the bakers of Pompeii: *Paquius Proculus* (I 7, 7), who exported bread as far away as rival Nocera!! In order to win over the clientele, the bread had to be of the best quality and baked to perfection, ready to be given hot to the patrons of the nearby Stabian thermal baths, *Sittius'* Tavern (VII 1 , 44) and the idle citizens who passed their days at the *Quadrivium* of the *Holconii*. Even on that hot day in August, Modesto was working like a dog on the last batch of the day: from dawn, even before the sun soaked the roofs and streets of Pompeii, servants, men and women kneaded the flour ground on the day before. The bread rose well on the kneading boards, it was the bread of masters, made from super-

fine flour! 81 round loaves were divided into segments and made according to the weight established by the *aedilis*. Modesto was thinking proudly that he could now start to have his own brand, like one of his self-important rivals. The air was thick and still and the dog started to howl strangely. Suddenly a loud rumble could be heard that made the walls and roof of the house tremble, a black haze was seen over Mt. Vesuvius and a hail of small stones started to fall. With pillows over their heads, the workers and clients fled, while the bread, protected by the oven, continued to cook for a long time, in vain, darkening over the centuries. Almost 1800 years later, an archaeologist, removing the layer of lava fragments and ash, found the carbonized bread still whole: imagining it to be overcooked baked goods...

34. *Castellum Aquae* in Pompeii: the story of *Marcus Attilius Primus*

I would like to talk about the Castellum Aquae in Pompeii for two very good reasons. The first is because of how it worked: it is one of the greatest works

of hydraulic engineering ever made to supply water to a city! Located near Porta Vesuvio at the highest point of Pompeii (42 m), water was collected into it from a branch of the Serino aqueduct built by Augustus. From here, the water travelled through lead pipes underneath the sidewalks, reaching the hydraulic towers located at the intersections of the streets, and was spread across the city. The new water

system marked a turning point in the daily habits of the Pompeiians: prior to its creation, they had used rainwater that was gathered into a basin in the atrium (*impluvium*) after it passed through a hole in the roof and then flowed into an underground cistern, from where it was drawn out with buckets from the well. The *Castellum* allowed all Pompeiians to benefit from an abundant supply of fresh water

flowing out of the 40 public fountains and the wealthy could even have afforded to have private baths or a *nymphaeum*! The second reason to speak about the *Castellum Aquae* is because of the famous novel by Richard Harris from which a TV mini-series was also created. On August 22, 79 AD, a young hydraulic engineer, *Marcus Attilius Primus* was sent from Rome to assume the role of *aquarius*, or superintendent of the gigantic aqueduct that supplied Pompeii and eight other cities in the Gulf of Naples with water. All of this was organized quickly after the mysterious disappearance of his predecessor and *Marcus Attilius* realizes that for the first time ever, the water in the great Miseno cistern was gradually decreasing and becoming mixed with sulfur! Determined to solve the crisis before a revolt from the city, *Attilius* enlists the help of Admiral Pliny The Elder, moving to the slopes of the volcano in search of the source of the problem. As he unknowingly moves towards the heart of a nightmare, he discovers a scam, organized by the freedman *Numerius Popidius Ampliatus*, to supply cheap water to Pompeii by stealing funds intended for the tax collector ... I won't tell you the end of the story, just describe the final scene: *Marcus Attilius* and *Corelia*, the young Pompeiian daughter of *Ampliatus*, fleeing the hail of lava fragments through the deserted tunnels of the *Castellum Aquae* of Pompeii devastated by the catastrophe of the eruption... happy reading!

35. A normal working day in Pompeii...

What was a normal working day in Pompeii like? To take advantage of the daylight, it started at dawn and even if craft associations dictated

that there could only be eight working hours, luxury goods dealers were open until the late evening for some customers. Goldsmiths, jewelers, and silversmiths were profitable occupations in Pompeii, their workshops were full of stones, gems, knives, and burins. For personal hygiene and care, there were perfumers, whose headquarters were located in the North side of *Macellum* (market), on Via degli Augustali, but there were also makeup artists, barbers, and combers. The streets were overrun by signs, benches, awnings, baskets and goods. A hard-working crowd was busy with even more physical activities: shoemakers, leather tanners, bronzeworkers, carpenters, masons, ceramicists, and painters. The textile industry was very prosperous: in the *officinae lanifricariae*, the beating and washing of raw wool took place; in the *officinae textoriae*, wool was spun and woven; in *tinctoriae*, fabrics were dyed and given color. At the doors of the workshops, movers, equipped with wagons or mules, were waiting to distribute goods all over the city. There is even evidence of doctors at Pompeii: near the Large *Palaestra*, there was an "emergency clinic" for accidents that happened during gymnastic or gladiatorial exercises. At night *scriptores*, professional writers, painted the walls of the city with electoral propaganda or announcements of gladiator performances. Other temporary professions included wizards who took advantage of ingenuity to sell potions and amulets to gullible clients. Artists were also considered simple craftsmen: they come from the lower classes and were often foreigners. At the lowest level of society were the slaves: you could buy them in the Forum just as any other object, they were displayed on a stage with a card in their hand or sign around their neck containing their personal data and capabilities. In the city, slaves were engaged in domestic work; the most educated of them were used for the master's accounting or the education of their children.

36. The guard at Porta Ercolano

This story is a lot of fun and explains how many "urban legends" are born. It takes place at Porta Ercolano. The monumental entrance, restored after the earthquake,

is made up of three openings, the two side arches were reserved for pedestrians and the central one, the largest, was used for wagons heading to Oplontis, Herculaneum and Naples. Exit from the small arch on the left and get onto Via dei Sepolcri where the charming necropolis begins. You will immediately notice an adjoining structure to the gate with a large rectangular niche. This monument has inspired the imagination of many people and even created an urban legend that, originating as a story told by tour guides, soon became so entrenched in the city's literature that it was reported in the account of a tour of Pompeii in 1869. The legend explains that the niche would have been the seat of the guard in charge of the gate of the city, and inside it was found the skeleton of the fearless legionary left in charge of protecting the city on that unlucky day in 79 AD. According to the story,

the soldier, faithful to his duty, stood perfectly still with his spear in his hand in the place he was supposed to guard and not even the rain of lava fragments and ash managed to tear him from his moral duty. The moving story of the "disciplined legionary martyr" was reported in numerous diaries and tales of Pompeii up until the mid-20 century. The story was still told even though in 1884 the monument was actually identified as the niche of the Augustan official, *Marcus Cerinnius Restitutus*, whose epigraph, discovered near the building, tells us that it was built by the decree of De-curions (city meeting) at the expense of the city. But we all know that people love to tell and hear about passionate

stories, so even you can pretend that this is the sentry box of the last man who saw Pompeii die.

37. The *fullonica* (fullery) of *L. Veranius Hypsaeuxs*

What was an elegantly-dressed lady in a green, fashionable chiton doing in *L. Veranius*

Hypsaeus' fullonica (fullery) (VI, 8, 2)? One of the maids was showing her a piece of green cloth, it was a very fashionable color; the owner *L. Veranius Hypsaeus* was describing to her the magnificence of his business, but she was puzzled ... She was not there for a new dress, but to find cloth coverings for the walls of her summer *triclinium* decorated with floral elements, masks and motifs inspired by Egyptian decorations which would enrich the sumptuous borders just like on real walls! This new "ornamental style" that had replaced the previous complex architecture was now so common that everyone was talking about it. Her *domus* could certainly not be any less ele-

gant than that of *M. Lucretius Fronto* (V 4, 11) who had recently had his redecorated with landscapes and idyllic villas to show that he was a candidate worthy of being an *aedilis* (city magistrate)! Creating the tapestry would be difficult work for her and her maids in centering and sewing together the neutral fabric panels in an elegant pattern with the more detailed ones on which the *pictores imaginarii* (work creators) had let their imagination have free rein… These drapes, linens and precious damask fabrics, which were completely incinerated by the eruptive fury of 79 AD, would have been found in the house swelling in the summer breezes, retaining the warmth of the convivial joy that arose in the winter, or surprisingly letting off aromas of spices and hints of essences perhaps purchased from the well-equipped House of the Garden of Hercules (Perfumers). But let's go back to our lady in the fullery: the fabric did not convince her, it was not the one she sought. Someone had told her about the textile workshop of *Verecundus* (IX 7, 5) and the nickname "decent" that fit him like a glove, like the shoes he sold along with the beautiful fabrics he produced. She would go and try his shop on Via dell'Abbondanza: the main street that was an absolute "must" for shopping!

38. Naevoleia Tyche and Munatius Faustus: a Pompeiian love story

There was a special tomb in Pompeii in the most traditional cemetery outside Porta Ercolano

normally reserved for aristocratic families or rich *mercatores* (merchants). The tomb is strange because it was not actually a grave, but a simple "celebratory monument", as those that were mentioned in the epitaph were alive when it was built and subsequently buried in a much smaller funeral area in another necropolis at Porta Nocera. The long inscription on the façade informs viewers that the tomb was built by a rich freedwoman *Naevoleia Tyche* for *C. Munatius Faustus*, one of the priests of

the cult of Augustus. The monument contained all the clichés found in the decadent burial of the rich freedman *Trimalchio* so ironically described by *Petronius*, including bas-reliefs with *bisellium* (seats of honor for two people), social recognition of the community, and a cargo ship that, in addition to being well-outfitted for its final voyage, was used as a reminder of *Munatius Faustus'* business activities. Aside from all this, the tomb that was not a tomb was a grand public confession, an expression of love by

the freedwoman for *Faustus* that was so great that she would follow him even into death. We have seen many expressions of love confessed by Pompeiian women, but this example is particular: she was a freedwoman, rich, admired, and an entrepreneur; he was a man in the public eye, one of Augustus' priest, who was granted his office by the community and even the honor of the *bisellium* by the Decurions: so why then was this tomb so strange? Because *Faustus* was not *Naevoleia's* husband. Proof of this fact comes from the absence of the possessive "her" in the epigraph, which would have accompanied the recipient's name, and the fact that she spoke distinctly of her liberties as well of *Faustus'* liberties, showing that she did not belong to the family of her beloved. *Naevoleia*, a well-known businesswoman of the time, pronounced her love publicly via a sepulchral monument, a passionate love that did not fear what people would say! A love that gave meaning to the phrase *"united in life and death"*!

39. Pompeii and *peplum*-movies (sword-and-sandal)

Did you know that the world of cinema has been interested in Pompeii since the very beginning and never really ceased to be so?

Starting in 1908, Arturo Ambrosio, owner of the largest Italian film production company of the time, decided to create a film from the novel written in 1834 by Bulwer-Lytton, *"The Last Days of Pompeii"*. The storyline centered on the love affair between Glaucus and Ione, around which all of Pompeian society of the time circled: gamblers, poets, gladiators, priests, and slaves all in the context of the eruption. The movie, a *peplum* (sword-and-sandal) movie icon, was exported all over the world, receiving great public and critical success. Its huge success gave birth to numerous remakes: in 1913, two versions were made at the same time that were both highly appreciated; the remake of the historical colossal film in 1926 succeeded in saving Italian cinema from a moment of great crisis; one of the numerous other best-selling versions was made in 1959 and included Sergio Leone among its screenwriters! Hollywood's *"The Last Days of Pompeii"*, made in 1935, has a gladiatorial-religious background and is unrelated to Bulwer-Lytton's

STEVE REEVES - CRISTINE KAUFFMAN - BARBARA CARROLL - ANNEMARIE BAUMANN

GLI ULTIMI GIORNI DI POMPEI

MIMMO PALMARA - FERNANDO REY - CARLO TAMBERLANI
ANGEL ARANDA - GUILLERMO MARIN

novel. The film, absurd in its historical approach and with inadequate special effects, was a resounding failure. This was not the case for *"Les derniers jours de Pompei"*, a French-Italian co-production directed at Cinecittà in 1948 with suggestive imagery and the spectacular eruption of Mt. Vesuvius, one of the most important cinematic successes of the time. In 1984, an Italian-American production company produced a TV-series of *"The Last Days of Pompeii"* with high-caliber actors such as Laurence Oliver and Franco Nero. In 2007, Raiuno broadcast a two-episode miniseries titled *"Pompeii"* which was part of the series known as *"Imperium"* based on the lives of the Roman emperors. In October 2010, the first scene was shot for the 3D film *"In search of the treasure of Pompeii"*. In 2007, Polanski collaborated with writer Robert Harris, author of the famous novel *"Pompeii"*, to write the screenplay for a film for the big screen. The cast of actors to be considered included Orlando Bloom, playing the part of *Marcus Attilius*, and Scarlett Johansson as his female counterpart, but because of a screenwriter strike, the production was suspended and subsequently cancelled definitively. In 2010, part of this footage and material became part of a 4-hour miniseries produced by Ridley Scott. In the end, Pompeii, suddenly frozen in time on a day in 79 AD like a huge photograph, has always been an inexhaustible source for any and all possible, correct or distorted, reconstructions of ancient civilization.

40. What was there to eat in Pompeii?

What did food look like on a normal day in Pompeii?

If a good day really began in morning, then a Pompeiian had to entrust his liver to the protection of the local goddess, the protector of food, *Carna*! In fact, Pompeiians' jaws starting working early at dawn with "*ientaculum*", a hearty breakfast of bread and cheese, fruit and meat, often containing leftovers from dinner the night before. Then a quick walk to work it off and open up their shop or go to the Forum to hear the news; or maybe a quick trip to the *tonsor* (barber) with a comment on the candidates or the elections of the *duoviri* (the main city magistrates). Mornings passed like this, while the smells that came from peddlers and the *thermopolia* become more and more irresistible, and at mid-day, it was time for a snack: large, tasty sausages; olives in brine, special because they come from the Lattari Mountains; various types of bread and

biscuits; ricotta "fuscella" (a sophisticated delicacy still popular today); unmistakable blue fish marinated or fried in batter; wild boar or pork sausage and then the usual drink at Asellina's *Caupona* (tavern). Then came the last buyers or clients, rushing to do their final errands before the shops closed, a chat at the baths and then home for the main meal! It was usually made up of an appetizer and a main dish, and then they were off to bed this was the typical "dinner" of a Pompeiian. But on special occasions, when friends and neighbors came over, you knew when dinner would start, but not when it would end, from the appetizer all the way to dessert! The beginning was marked by the "*gustum*" or "*gustatio*" (taster). The eggs were sacred and untouchable, served with a side dish of all the vegetables and fresh produce taken from the home *hortus* (garden).

After the appetizer, the meal passed to the first course (*prima mensae*), with the best dish being fish, especially fried, cold or hot, with giant oysters drowned in scented lemons from far away *Surrentum*. And if the banquet was particularly lavish, there would also have been various meats offered at the table, not only those of hunting animals, but also of game found in abundance on Mt. Vesuvius and the Lattari mountains, and exotic dishes made from cranes, flamingos, parrots and peacocks! Finally, the time arrived for desserts (*secundae mensae*), with dinners' thirst quenched by an abundance of *Falernum*, a wine that Bacchus created by transforming the slopes of the Massico into lush vineyards. The evening continued with a symposium in which wine was served - always watered down - accompanied by some food, such as leeks, that stimulated the desire to drink. Then, after the obligatory "show" of the *conviva eructans* (guests burping), to confirm their pleasure in the dinner, everyone went home taking their *mappa*, a napkin with the evening's leftovers, anticipating the following morning's breakfast. The next day, the cycle started all over again...

41. Empress Poppaea Sabina at Pompeii

The story of Emperor Nero's ambitious and unscrupulous second wife, *Poppaea Sabina,* is intertwined

with that of Pompeii. Her family came from one of the neighboring areas, as is demonstrated by the numerous houses in the city only a couple dozen meters from each other all owned by the *Poppaei.* Among them is the House of Pansa (VI 6, 1), that of the Golden Cupids (VI 16, 7), and the majestic building over 2000 m² known as the House of Menander (I 10, 4), belonging to Sabina's uncle, *Quintus Poppaeus Secundus.* This man, who used to paint his nails gold-colored, was so famous that it was enough to say *fulbunguis* (the manicured hand with the reddish-brown nails), a nickname that we find in an inscription painted on the outer wall of the house, to understand who it was talking about. There are many examples of graffiti on the walls of Pompeii showing affection for *Poppaea Sabina,* who only a few years after marrying Nero, had become the new Empress of Rome. *"May you always be allowed to prosper, Sabina, and stay young forever."* Her enemies, on the other hand, were also numerous and did not let any opportunity pass to emphasize harshly *"Sabina, you are not doing well".* Even on the walls of one of the rooms of the aforementioned House of Menander, there is a greeting for *Claudia Octavia,* the first wife of Nero, who was killed so

that he could marry the beautiful Pompeiian... One of the signs of *Poppaea*'s goodwill towards her city was sending them a unique gift: a gold lamp of extraordinary size and value which was delivered by her relatives to the Sanctuary of Pompeiian Venus in 64 AD. Compatible with her other worldly commitments, the divine *Poppaea* could be seen with a certain frequency at the luxurious *Oplontis* villa, a well-known bath complex just outside of Pompeii. Here, set amongst the green of the slopes of

Mt. Vesuvius and the blue of the Gulf of Naples, lived the "jet set" of Imperial Rome. The Empress could find the time and pleasure here to have a swim in the sea, another in the great Olympic pool and another, perhaps, in a mythical bath of donkey's milk! The villa was made up of more than 100 rooms, modulated by grand, refined architecture and enriched with greatly artistic colorful wall paintings. It is here that it is said that Divine *Poppaea* found death in the eruption of 79 AD: having been abandoned by all her slaves, she could not escape the fury of the volcano!! And even though it is true that the excavations in the villa have not recovered her skeleton, legend says that the Imperial carriage was found still inside the house ...

42. Selling shoes

From the *atrium of Praedia* by Julia Felix (II, 4, 3) comes this scene of shoes for sale, which today can be seen at the Archaeological Museum of Naples,

testimony to a lively, folkloristic trade in the streets of Pompeii. A salesman proudly shows off how well the shoes are stacked, while in the "shop", business is in full swing! Close to a porch (maybe that of the Forum), we find a scene that was common in the neighborhoods of Naples until a few decades ago: a man, the owner himself, kneels to serve a customer by putting their shoe on, while a young boy seems to be respectfully waiting nearby. From the liveliness of the acts and the gestures of the characters, it almost seems as if you can hear the voices on that street from that time: *"No! He doesn't take a 44, but a 43 ½ to be precise."* Would the client have bought those shoes? Do those sizes still exist today? They were all local handicrafts, all handmade! And for the ladies? Or sandals for slaves? The remaining part of the frieze shows a small sketch on the right with a person seated holding a *tabula scriptoria*, one of those tablets that could be etched into using a stylus to record someone's thoughts or those of another. The person gazes upwards suggesting that he is lost in

thought, perhaps intent on reproducing the design of the equestrian statue that he sees (a fine arts student?), or instead listening to the demands of the person right in front of him. In that case, he would have been a traveling writer, perhaps paid for writing a love letter or some other correspondence for a poorly educated client. And we could even ask ourselves why the owner of this large hotel-house, owner of the strange sign outside *"for rent: an elegant bathroom for decent people, workshops with homes above, apartments on the first floor"*, had scenes of every part of daily life in Pompeii painted in his atrium. Was it another way to attract customers? Pompeiians sold shoes, drew images, played music in the streets, got drunk, cursed, loved, studied, were lazy, sang, bought and sold items, emptied and filled containers, called on the gods, walked and stopped to admire the view just like any city today. What makes it extraordinary is that it is a city of yesterday, indeed, many yesterdays ago ... that has never stopped pulsating with life!

43. House of the Sarno Lararium

It is such a small *lararium* that it almost risks being passed by unnoticed, this *sacellum* dedicated to the deities of the household

which gave its name to the house of the same name, known as the House of the Sarno Lararium (I, 14, 7). Like all those looking over the bustling Via di Castricio, the dwelling is modest and would have been inhabited by workers or small entrepreneurs connected to their trades and "heirs" of the rich citizens who were displaced after the earthquake of 62 AD. The niche, located at the end of the corridor following the *atrium*, is of a disconcerting simplicity compared to other much more lavish *lerariums* (that of the nearby House of Menander for example), but it is charming, even containing a small moat around it that could be filled with water to resemble the course of the Sarno river. The part that makes this *lararium* special is the subject that is painted on it: a journey on the Sarno that in ancient times must have been navigable, at least until the eruption in 79 AD, when the total disruption of the river's course forced the loss of its hydrographic recognition for a long time. But why did the client choose this theme for his household shrine? The god of the Sarno river looks very focused on his work of pouring water from a vessel into the canal below, which in turn feeds the river, and seems to be stoically indifferent to what is happening on the other side of the scene. A boat can be seen filled

with unspecified food products (perhaps olives), with two mules and two sailors aboard; further on, three men are on the ground, passing a basket to each other; two other small figures on the right are weighing baskets on a scale that they hang on the stairs. The only character dressed in a long tunic, the *dominus* (master), is intent on directing and supervising the work of the others. It is the representation of an entire household with numer-

ous slaves who ask for the protection of the Lari, the gods of the house, to whom they make daily sacrifices. The gods of the family and the god of the river Sarno are the creators of the success and well-being of the whole house: the *dominus* (master) owns a boat, two mules, six slaves and is the owner of a small agricultural venture that also creates produce for the markets in nearby cities! His pride could also be found in the grateful demeanor of those slaves who could see themselves daily in the household shrine beside their respectable *dominus* (master) in a rare moment of mutual affection!

44. *Aulus Umbricius Scaurus: garum* manufacturer

How many times have you heard *garum* being spoken about? In Pompeii, the best *garum* was sold by *Aulus Umbricius Scaurus,*

who also advertised it on the mosaic of the *atrium* of his home, constructed panoramically straddling the ancient city walls!! The famous trader had the four corners of the *impluvium* constructed as ampoules used for storage of the sauces with his name "*Scaurus*" and the expression "*liqua(minis) flos*", "super-fine waste" written on them. There are different varieties of *garum*, from that with the thickest sauce that was less precious, to that which was more watery and refined. Apicio, who mentions a series of ancient recipes, does not talk about the one for *gar-um* as its preparation was taken for granted. It was ubiquitous on the Roman table, used to flavor meat, chicken, lamb and vegetables! The sauce was obtained from the fermentation of entrails of different kinds of fish (sardines, anchovies, red mullet, and sea bass to which were added tuna, mackerel, sturgeon and eels), salted beforehand and sun-dried, then marinated in garlic, mint, laurel, celery, fennel seeds, black pepper and finally with a spray of vinegar. The Pompeians preferred the sauce "very watery" served in drops as a true elixir and of

which they became the foremost producers and exporters. At the beginning of his career, *Umbricius*, a great supporter of the gladiatorial games, successfully used a number of strategies to sell his goods. Enriched with the "gold from fish", he moved into a new, luxurious house equipped with a peristyle, vast gardens, large rooms and a workshop for the production of *garum*. Carts loaded with fish were delivered to the courtyard to wait to be treated. Six partially buried semicircular jars were left behind, covered with terracotta covers, still full of precious *liquamen*. In the garden behind the house, an abundance of surplus rounded amphorae of various shapes were found, waiting to be filled, and even funnels that had already been used. *Umbricius' garum* was the best in the area around Rome and was exported to many parts of the Mediterranean. As a result of this successful

trade, *Umbricius* reached a very high level on the social and economic scale of the city, so much so that in Nero's era, he earned the title of *duovir*!

"You use fat fish like sardines and mackerel and then another 1/3 portion of various other fish. You need a large capacity tank of about thirty liters in size. On the very bottom of the tank, make a layer of dried herbs with strong spices such as dill, coriander, fennel, celery, mint, pepper, saffron, and oregano. On top of this layer, place the entrails and small fish whole, while those of larger fish should be cut into pieces. Above this, spread a layer of salt two-fingers deep. Repeat the layers until you reach the rim of the container. Allow the mixture to rest for seven days. Mix it often for a few more days. In the end, a rather dense liquid is obtained, "*garum*". It can be preserved for a long time."

Recipe by *Marcus Valerius Martialis*.

45. Why did Pompeii need a smaller theater?

Many people will have asked themselves this question and many others will also know the answer. The *Odeon* was a small roofed theater that

could host a limited, refined audience of about 1,300 people for performances of poetry recitals accompanied by the sound of the harpsichord and mime shows. It was built next to the Large Theater after the foundation of the colony of Pompeii (80 BC), at the initiative of the *duoviri Caius Quinctius Valgus* and *Marcus Porcius,* the same officials who built the Amphitheater. What

many do not know is that on the plaster coating of the exterior walls of the theatrical complex, there are numerous examples of graffiti left by the ancient visitors as a reminder of their passage! These were people that had come from far away; a group of inscriptions is even in Safaitic, a pre-Islamic language!! There are beautiful verses signed by a certain *Tiburtinus*, who, inspired by the

love stories of the mimes, wrote: *"If you know what love is, if you recognize yourself as a human being, have mercy on me, let me come to you...."* In mimes, the actors presented the noteworthy parts of a short text that was read aloud and accompanied by music. The mimes recited without masks and had bare feet, and it was the only performance that women could also take part in. Just like today, actors were true celebrities, received special honors and were entitled to citizenship. An epigraph from Purpureo's tavern gives evidence for the presence of *"paridiani"*, fans of the actor Paris, a successful performer that was also mentioned by Tacitus. Another pantomime was a master of Vesuvian scenes, *Actius Anicetus*, with his own theater company and fan-club, the *Actiani Anicetiani*. And one of the few, if not only, portrait of burlesque actresses (*Atellanae*) that comes to us from antiquity is from the Temple of Isis of Pompeii. It is the bronze bust of *Caius Norbanus Sorex*, mentioned by Plutarch as the favorite actor of the Dictator Silla.

46. *Numerius Popidius Celsinus* and Isis

It is said that it was a visit to the temple of Isis, rediscovered at Pompeii during excavations in 1764, that influenced the fertile imagination of fourteen-year-old

Mozart, giving him the inspiration, twenty-one years later, for the choreography of *The Magic Flute*. And a few decades later, after the discovery of the temple in Pompeii, it served as the inspiration for an almost identical reconstruction, the so-called "Roman Temple", incorporated into the English Garden of the Royal Palace of Caserta. As it was, the discovery in Pompeii of the first true Egyptian temple, full of references to the Nilotic world and the ancient civilization of the Pharaohs, which had not yet been discovered, created a great sensation and interest in the well-known travelers of the time! The original construction of the temple dates back to the 2nd century BC but it was completely razed to the ground by the earthquake in 62 AD and restored thanks to the financial intervention of a shrewd, enterprising freedman: *Numerius Popidius Ampliatus*. This *parvenu* (upstart) did not fail to make his prodigality public via a gigantic inscription on the architrave of the entrance of the building. It can therefore be said that, just like today, wealth meant power: the generosity shown by *Ampliatus* to the city earned his son, *Numidius Popidius Celsinus*, only six years old, access to the Senate as a citizen. Lacking discretion, *Numidius Popidius Celsinus* paraded together with priests and priestesses of worship in a symbolic procession paint-ed on the walls of the fenced porch surrounding the temple. Another procession that became famous for its richness and its splendor took place on March 5 in honor of the goddess Isis. At the end of winter, the goddess, protector of sailors, was brought to the beach where her ship was put out to sea carrying a propitiatory prayer to rediscover navigation. The Temple of Isis in Pompeii was struck by the eruption during one of the fullest moments of its functionality: at the time of discovery, the main altar of the sanctuary was full of the ashes and burnt bones of animal victims offered to the goddess!

47. "I wouldn't sell my husband for all the gold in the world"

The owner of this Pompeian home was truly lucky, even if it is less well-known than others because of its state of devastation.

It is made special by the love that it was home to before the catastrophe! That the dwelling belonged to *D. Caprasius Primus* (VII 2, 48) is revealed by the sign with his name found in one of the rooms facing the *atrium*: a wine-seller with a beautiful house, but above all with a loving wife, as can be seen from the graffiti *virum vendere nolo meum quanta quantique* ("I wouldn't sell my husband for all the gold in the world"). There is an awareness of feelings in this woman from 2000 years ago that is much closer to the modern way of conceiving and feeling love than was usually seen in Rome and elsewhere, where almost every conjugal union was affected by intrigues and affairs.

Here, on the slopes of Mt. Vesuvius, you could breathe the air of true harmony! The "modern" feel of this Pompeian dedication confirms the uniqueness of the person being loved and the sweet awareness that they could not love anyone else. Nothing could interfere with the heart's reasoning, and with the touching *"quanta quantique"*, a woman confides the value of irreplaceability of her beloved. Was it a question of social class? Yes, perhaps that was the case, the higher you went in class, the more the calculation of perspectives of gain in the long- and medium-term outweighed agreements made for political ends, dowry, or social prestige. In Pompeii, where the population was further from the center of power, love expressed on the city walls was as almost as frequent as that found in the lines of *Catullus*. One might argue that on this wall of the *domus* of *Caprasius Primus*, VII 2, 48, we do not read about a lifetime, but rather a day of love, and not a poem, but a verse: but it was just enough to make this anonymous wife synonymous with conjugal love!

> *VIRUM VENDERE NOLO MEUM QUANTA QUANTIQUE*

48. A day at the *Macellum* (market) of Pompeii

Access via two open entrances on the eastern porch of the Forum of Pompeii led to the *Macellum*, the permanent market set up in the city.

The wall surrounding the large colonnaded courtyard was restored and redecorated after suffering earthquake damage with paintings featuring mythological scenes and still lifes with birds and fish. The fish pictured were the same ones that were cleaned and sold in the twelve-sided pavilion in the middle of the building supported by wooden poles anchored with stones! Fish vendors always had counters made of precious, hard stone, as they needed them to be clean and maintain good hygiene. But the *Macellum* was not only a fish market, it was also home to other commercial activities found in small shops for food products located along the southern side, an auction room, or under the portico occupied by the money-changers. Another function of the building was its religious one: in the three *sacelli* (shrines) along the bottom side where statues of the Flavian dynasty have been found, visitors practiced the cult of the dynasty of the Emperor, officiated by the *ministri augustales* (Augustus' priests). But come on, let's go to the market to buy fish today! In the general confusion of people shouting,

sellers inviting customers to see the merchandise, and people sliding on the wet floor, we approach the central *tholos* (small round building), where the best fish are on display. A man next to us, also attracted by the wonderful goods, asks the fish seller for the price, and is told that it is 50 *assi*! He refuses, and gets it for 20 *assi*. The man who has just bought the fish is met by a guy who identifies himself as his old friend. This newcomer, a man of athletic build, greets him warmly and hugs and kisses him with affection. From the words that they exchange, we understand that this is the city's *aedilis*, a magistrate responsible for the rations and price control. The *aedilis*, showing off his power to his friend, chastises the fisherman, who in his opinion has sold a poor product at an exaggerated price!

49. A Pompeiian column in Japan

With its more than three million visitors per year (equivalent to an annual revenue of about 30 million Euros!), it is well-known that Pompeii is the most visited archaeological site in the world.

That the lion's share of this business is produced by foreigners and, to a large extent, by the Japanese, is also commonly known. And finally, that Pompeiian archaeological finds have often gone on tour around the world as part of exhibitions before hastily being returned home, is not new to anyone. But there is a unique story of a monument from Pompeii which is found in Japan which is worth telling. The story begins on August 23, 1868 in Japan, when the country was torn apart by a bloody civil war. The "White Tiger Regiment" (called *Byakkotai*), a handful of about 20 samurai between the ages of 15 and 17, after losing a battle, preferred to commit collective suicide rather than to surrender. This is where Pompeii enters into the story. In 1928, Mussolini became aware of this ritual suicide and decided to make it an *exemplum* of virtue and fidelity. To bear witness to his admiration, he dedicated a Roman column from Pompeii (topped with a bronze eagle) in their honor. The gift was especially appreciated and the Pompeiian column, locat-

ed on the Limori hill where the 20 young people are buried, is cleaned every morning and even today, is celebrated annually with a big party. On the Carrara marble base of the column-cenotaph can be read: "*As a symbol of the fascists, Rome, the mother of all civilizations, with this millennial column, testimony of eternal greatness, pays Imperial tribute to the memory of the heroes of Biaccotai. The year MCMXXVIII VI was fascist.*" On another side, a poem is engraved "*No matter how many people have washed the stones with their tears, these names will never disappear from the world.*"

50. The textile workshop of *Marcus Vecilius Verecundus*

Via dell'Abbondanza was home to the textile workshop of *Verecundus*: it fabricated cloth, felt objects and textiles used to make knitwear, tunics,

cloaks and ribbons. The workshop was in the front of a building that *Verecundus* had previously used for another trade, before transforming himself from an innkeeper into a fuller. He had a bad character and was very attached to money, but knew the best places where flax and hemp were grown, the procedure for how to wash fabrics with ash and soapstones, and was a master at working linen made from Scotch broom: truly stylish! As a "mordant" for dyeing fabrics, he used Egyptian potassium and for ammonia, he discreetly collected the urine of passersby, as was customary at the time. For dyes, he used turmeric and henna, but did not turn his nose up at dyeing wool in tufts and maple was no stranger to him. *Verecundus* created warm colors from yellow to brown, as well as shades between the primary colors in beautiful pastels from pink, extracts from hollyhock, to green, obtained from chamomile flowers. His sign alone was a guarantee to everyone for all that it had cost him! It took up an entire wall protected by a special awning and depicted the Pompeiian *Venus* on a chariot in the shape of the bow of the ship drawn by four beautiful elephants! The images of the goddess *Fortuna* and the god *Genius* could be seen on the sides, and below, the advertisement for his fullery. From comb finishing to fabrics passing from the dyeing to the packaging of the product, his self-portrait was found everywhere including the slogan: *M(arcus) Vecilius Verecundus vestiar(ius)*, as if saying "by *Marcus Vecilius*, the respectable tailor". The showroom of the Pompeiian designer was obviously the best that could be asked for in terms of elegance and the beauty of the fabrics; clients left his workshop dressed to the nines!! And the beautiful awning, already mentioned, created shade over the entrance and surrounding area, allowing ladies to admire the fabrics they had bought after they left without getting wet in bad weather or getting too hot when the sun shone brightly!

51.The ship Europa

The walls of Pompeii are the best witnesses of daily life where the signs or designs of

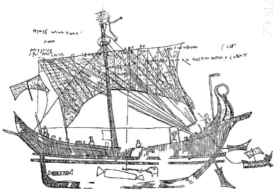

a sometimes childish, sometimes adult hand, carved with a knife or any sharp nail can be seen. The most beautiful graffiti ever made was engraved on the north wall of the peristyle of a house situated at the crossroads of Via dell'Abbondanza (I, 15, 3). The drawing shows a large transport ship navigating with its sails open towing a lifeboat, also equipped with a sail. There are many structural details of the hull and equipment visible and even the name of the ship can be seen attached to a sign above the cutwater line. The ship was called *Europa*, like the Greek heroin kidnapped at sea by *Jupiter* disguised as a bull. About the drawing, not done either by a boy nor an amateur, not much is known, but it is likely that the author was a ship owner, a naval engineer or in some way an artisan of navigation, as the graffiti gives us an exact likeness of how a ship was structured in 79 AD. A curious note is the presence on the ship "Europa" of a sort of hollow, or niche, or who knows what kind of strange object drawn on the scaffolding of the stern, in front of the probable cabin of the commander, and whose exact purpose remained unclear for a long time. The answer finally came from excavations made on an ancient ship wreck: at exactly that point of the stern, a marble altar with

a bronze lamp, columns and various bellows was discovered. The graffiti from Pompeii then became clear: the good sailor had drawn everything that ancient ships had on board, even the altar. How many other parts are still unknown? Ships have always been the highest expression of the degree of technological knowledge of a people at any time in civilization. If our future ancestors from the year 5000 explore the shipwreck of the Andrea Doria, even without using other sources, they would be able to get accurate information about what Italians knew and were able to do around the mid-20th century: metallurgy, hydrodynamics, electronics, mechanics, meteorology, power, economics, trade, and religion ... on a large ship, you can find everything: a complete overview of civilization and science!

52. Women in Pompeii

Walking through the streets of Pompeii, in a place still strangely alive, one wonders what life was like for ancient Pompeiian woman. In Pompeii,

women were responsible for the well-being of the family and that of the home: they had to look after their children, supervise and monitor the work of slaves, prepare clothes, organize religious ceremonies, as well as check and see that there were adequate supplies and medicines for the household. Evidence from graffiti on the walls shows us that Pompeiian women participated in political life and electoral campaigns, even though they did not have the right to vote. Many women, especially those in the highest classes, attended private lessons and about 20% of women in the city knew how to read and write. Women held public religious offices, participated in the city's financial and commercial life, and were even entrepreneurs. But the typical Pompeiian *mundus muliebris* (worldly woman) also paid a lot of attention to beauty and numerous female portraits demonstrate women's desire to be portrayed at their best with jewelry made of gold and precious stones, ornaments or hairstyles that were "in" to better enhance their beauty. Oh how women can be! Body treatments involved depilation, the use of abrasive substances to eliminate impurities, and massages and creams made with various essential oils. Hair was styled with bone combs, brushes,

hairpins and sometimes even wigs. Hair could also be dyed using dyes made from plants. Facial details were highlighted with various colored eye shadows. And speaking of women, there is a tomb located in the Porta Nocera necropolis which contained verses on a funeral stele dedicated to a beautiful, elegantly dressed woman from her inconsolable husband: *"Dear stranger, I do not have much to tell you. Stop and read this. This is the not-so-beautiful tomb of a beautiful woman. Her parents called her Claudia. She loved her husband with all her heart. She raised two children. One of them she leaves behind, the other she has already buried. She spoke delightfully and walked with grace. She spun wool and took care of the house. I'm finished, you can go on your way."* How could that husband, devoted to the memory of his beautiful, pious Claudia, have ever known that the virtues of his wife would be known to foreign passersby almost 2000 years later?

53. Was Pulcinella at the Theater of Pompeii?

Did you know that the only genuinely original theatre genre that the Roman world produced

was invented in Campania? And that the performances of these shows occurred in the Theater of Pompeii? Comedy and tragedy can certainly not be considered inventions of the Romans, having been adopted in their entirety from Greece. But aside from these two literary forms, one other theater genre was very popular in Pompeii: the popular farce called *Atellana*. The name came from an obscure Oscan city called Atella where it had originated, and which was, in fact, in Campania. Although no text has survived from an *atellana* comedy, we

know that they were "intermezzos" based on fixed patterns and scenarios that were entrusted to improvisation just like in comedies! Standard characters with costumes and masks, long noses with prominent bellies, and ridiculous names (*Maccus*, the silly eater; *Pappus*, the stupid old man; *Buccus*, the bragging, petulant speaker; *Dossenus*, the smart hunchback or *Manducus*, a person chewing or grimacing) were given features that amused the audience, ready to laugh at any gluttony or drunkenness, noisy games and obscene jokes. At Pompeii, the *Atellanae* were fairly at home because they could be recited in the original Oscan language, still generally understood by the less fortunate social classes. An exceptional find from Pompeii provides evidence for a group of fifteen life-sized plaster masks used as models by an ancient craftsman to produce copies for the stage. Of note is the presence of a male mask of the typical comic character of the *atellana* farce, *Buccus*, as can be seen from the name that was imprinted in the fresh plaster. This character has a large nose that reminds us of someone ... oh, yes, it reminds us of Pulcinella's mask, although the latter is 1600 years more recent!

54. Where did Pompeiian children go to school?

So where did Pompeiian children go to school? So far, there has been no building found in the city or designated

in the city guides as a school. In Pompeii, like in Rome, there was no public school because teaching was not paid for by the state as it is today, and it was not even mandatory! Very wealthy families could afford a *pedagogus* (teacher), usually a Greek slave who taught boys from 6 to 16 years of age. We know of the *pedagogus, C. Iulius Elenus,* who held lectures in the *exedra* (a semi-circular area for a philosophical or other conversation) of the House of the Silver Wedding and

who, judging by the graffiti engraved by a schoolboy on the wall, was not exactly beloved!!! Those who did not have money for a private teacher were forced to hire a teacher who gave group lessons to their children. Teachers and tutors were not well-off: they were worse off than their pupils, paid with a miserly salary of eight asses monthly (their annual salary was equal to the prize earned in just one day by the winner of the circus games!). Maybe that's why they used the whip so of-

ten!! Near the Temple of Apollo, lessons were held by Master Sema who, like so many, took on the responsibility of educating children for a small sum from the families. The *ludimagister* (school teacher) gave lessons to his young students between the columns of the Forum, punishing them severely when needed: on the left, the good students sit on stools and hold waxed tablets (the notebooks of that time) on their knees. On the right, a bad student, leaning against his classmates' shoulders, gets a humiliating public whipping. There's nothing to be said, it was very strict education … The school of the teacher known as *Potitus* was instead frequented by "spoiled children". *Potitus* was a well-known, wealthy person who began teaching by renting a room on No-

lana Street, a small room that could hold about fifteen students. On the façade, writing in graffiti warned: *"silence, studying happens here! And you, lazybones, stop looking at the ceiling!"* It appears that *Potitus* also taught philosophy: on the wall of the classroom, a fresco depicted wisemen and philosophers with papyrus rolls in their hands. The teacher *Potitus* was represented at the center, a wise man among the wisemen!!!! The wealthy owner of the House of the Faun, and a wise expert of the field of law, took on the responsibility of teaching law in a room in his house, trying to help young practitioners get their start in in Forum life. His students had to learn rhetoric and oratory, two essential arts for future lawyers and legislators...

55. Ancient VIPs at Pompeii

On November 5, 44 BC, the weather in Pompeii was terrible. We know this from a letter from Marcus Tullius Cicero

addressed to a friend: *"As for me,"* writes the famous orator and politician from the 1st century BC, *"I holed up in my villa in Pompeii, as I wrote to you before, more than anything because of the bad weather: I have never seen a worse season."* And Cicero was right at home in Pompeii! In a neighborhood not far from the frenetic city center, just outside Porta Ercolano, maybe Cicero owned a beautiful piece of property with a comfortable, luxurious villa on it. It is said that Cicero participated in the siege of Pompeii in 89 BC along with Silla ... This villa is notable for the famous mosaic depicting street musicians holding a tibia, harpsichord and drum very similar to the one used in Neapolitan *tamurriate* (traditional songs)! Destiny chose this rich dwelling as one of the first to be struck by the hot ash cloud that fell on Pompeii on that morning in 79 AD. And it was also one of the first to be excavated on May 25, 1748. Cicero was not the only VIP from the an-

cient world to choose to buy a home in *Campania Felix*. It is said that *Drusus*, the son of Emperor *Claudius* from his first wife, *Plautia Urgulanilla*, died at Pompeii when he was four years old. This was bad luck following a tragic, stupid game: the young boy suffocated on a pear that he had thrown up into the air and swallowed whole to impress his friends. Another famous character from the era connected to Pompeii was the military tribune, *Titus Suedius Clemens*. The frenetic urban development of Pompeii after the damage caused by the earthquake in 62 AD had led to illegal construction activities on public lands by private individuals, causing numerous disputes. To restore order and give each owner his property back, often improperly built on by fraudulent third parties, Emperor *Vespasianus* sent the tribune *Titus Suedius Clemens* from Rome with extraordinary judicial powers to resolve the situation. His mandate was carved in memorial stones at the gates of the city: like a good soldier, he was not deterred by anything, even moving some of the tombs in the Porta Nocera neocropolis that had been built on public land!!

56. What did the Pompeiians look like?

We know a lot of things about Pompeiians; what they ate, how they lived, how they loved and

even how they died, but what did they look like, did their faces resemble ours? A beautiful portrait from Nero's era, depicting the features of two bourgeois spouses, their hairstyles, and even their gestures, perhaps can help us to unravel this mystery. The two are commonly referred to as "*Paquius Proculus* and his wife" because of an electoral propaganda poster painted outside the house supporting the candidature of *Paquius Proculus*, who was later elected as one of Pompeii's *duoviri*. Some others say that the poster actually refers to the rich baker *Terentius Neo* as writing in graffiti found inside the house seems to reveal. Beyond their social identity, the man in the portrait must have been the most influential citizen of the neighborhood. This is shown by the quality of his dwelling: the floor was a carpet of mosaics; at the entrance, there was a dog attached to a door knocker, while

style that was typical of Nero's age with her hair divided by a central part and gathered at the nape of the neck, except for some narrow curls that fall on her forehead. She shows off her high level of culture by holding a stylus to her lips, mimicking the iconographic style created for poets and muses. The man is dressed in the toga that identifies him as a Roman citizen and points to his rank as *magistratus* (magistrate), holding the *rotulus* (scroll) in clear view. Nevertheless, the standard traits, made by the author with the utmost fidelity, betray the provincial provenience of the two *parvenus* (upstarts), probably Samnites, who, having achieved economic prosperity, were fond of concealing their humble origins and sought to fully enter high society. The overall effect is unconvincing, almost as if it were a photomontage with silhouettes painted at a "carnival" and the result is exactly the opposite: the awkward pose of the wife and the crude and clumsy country roughness of the husband!

in the atrium, panels showed different animals. The two figures are portrayed as wealthy, refined, fashionable and stylish: the woman is wearing a red mantle, a pearl necklace with a gold pendant and pearl earrings, has a hair-

57. Giuseppe Garibaldi in Pompeii

From Bill Clinton to Leonardo Di Caprio, from Goethe to Pablo Picasso ... One of the many (and one of the first) famous

visitors to the excavations of Pompeii was the hero of the Two Worlds, Giuseppe Garibaldi. And among the many stories that come out of Pompeii that never cease to amaze us, there is also one about him, which acts as proof of the small contribution that this extraordinary archaeological site also played in the unification process of our country! It was September 12, 1860, and the "Expedition of the Thousand" to conquer the kingdom of the Two Sicilies was underway. Garibaldi had been in Naples as a liberator for only five days. The leader, driven by the intuitions of a European intellectual like Alessandro Dumas, immediately understood the political importance of the exceptional cultural heritage in Cam-

pania for the process of unification and building a national identity and consciousness. Therefore, with a decree signed as the dictator of southern Italy, he made the Museum of Naples and the excavations at Herculaneum and Pompeii national property, entrusting them to the Ministry of Education. A few days later, Garibaldi nominated his friend Dumas as the "honorary director" of the Pompeiian archaeological area, making a preliminary set of funds available to him to resume excavations and rectify the state of abandonment of the ancient city. On September 16, 1860, Garibaldi writes: *"Since the excavations of Pompeii have been miserably abandoned for many months causing torment to the academic world and with the harm that has been done by the surrounding populations and consid-* *ering the fact that our revolution must be truly Italian, worthy of a homeland filled with arts and research, I hereby decree that the excavations of Pompeii will become national property and will be given 5000 scudi (ecus) annually, and that excavation work must be immediately resumed…"* At that time, 22 hectares had been excavated and, by making a calculation, the sum allocated by Garibaldi was about 110,000 Euros (a shepherd earned 6 liras a month)! Today, 44 hectares have been excavated out of a total of 66 hectares. And the problems of managing such a large site continue to be worrying! After the signing of the decree on September 25, 1860, Giuseppe Garibaldi and his son visited the archaeological site of Pompeii; a Neapolitan photographer begged Garibaldi to stop for a picture and Garibaldi agreed.

58. The tomb of *Caius Vestorius Priscus*

The young magistrate *Caius Vestorius Priscus* who died in 75/76 AD at the age of 22 held the post of *aedilis* (the administrator for roads, buildings, and public order)

and was honored by the town council with a plot in the Porta Vesuvio necropolis to build his tomb and a sum of 2000 sesterces for the funeral which were given to his mother, *Mulvia Prisca*. These gifts were the motivation behind the determination of the matron to commemorate her son's social status. In the fenced area that enclosed the base and the altar, the young man represented frontally in an imposing stance as an official at a hearing is actually *Vestorius Priscus*. It was no coincidence that his mother chose this political celebration to commemorate

her son's memory, since the rank of a magistrate meant having achieved the social status of a bourgeois "as it should have been". Two gladiators are shown facing off, in memory of the games offered by the town council to honor his funeral, painted again to emphasize the ostentation of public recognition. Apart from these figures, a small table with a wonderful silver service was depicted, perfect in every detail and a sign of the ancient wealth of his home. The monumentalization of the funerary buildings expressed mutual competition and rank differ-

ences. It is also true that at the burial location, a funeral banquet was held that was symbolically offered to the gods and the deceased. And we know ever more about this. In many graves there was a duct connecting the earth with the urn in which the ashes of the deceased were found so that the libations offered during funeral ceremonies could reach them. The deceased were commemorated during *Parentalia* which lasted from February 13th to 21st and each family held a banquet at the tomb of their parents and other dead relatives, in a symbolic union with them.

59. *Publius Cornelius Faventinus,* the *tonsor* (barber)

Publius Cornelius Faventinus, the barber who opened his *tonstrina* (barbershop) near the Amphitheater under the porch of the Large Palaestra, really got a good

deal: people came there from all over Campania (Nola, Nocera, Acerra, Avella, Stabia, and Sorrento) to attend shows and, on normal days, the shade from the great plane trees even made many Pompeiians tempted to go for a walk ... A *tonsor* (barber) worked without stopping from dawn for eight solid hours (stopping around 1 o' clock) and there were plenty of customers, so much so that *Faventinus* even arranged stools and benches around his barbershop for those who had to wait. Waiting creat-

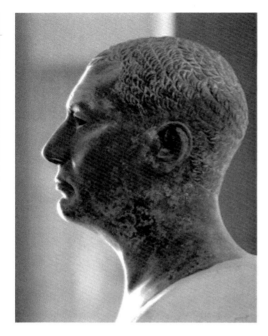

that was his specialty. The client followed the barber's moves anxiously, ready to run away because wounds were not that uncommon. The barber sprayed a lot of water on the customer's face, gave him a ball to put in his mouth to stretch out the skin of his cheek and for safety, always kept a concoction of cobwebs immersed in oil and vinegar to put immediately on any bleeding. At the end of the job, the customer was invited to look at himself in the large bronze mirror hanging on the wall. *Faventinus* was also a master at haircuts: he made real masterpieces with his iron scissors, created daring curls with the *calamistrum*, a hot piece of iron that was warmed under hot coals and, to round out his skills, could also create fake beauty marks with small circles of fabric, the fashionable *splenia lunata*. Some of you may not know that barbers were also expert beauticians: they performed cheek massages using ointments for those who wanted to hide a birthmark or liven up the color of their face. Their prices, shown in a special table, were proportional to their reputation, to the point that it was not surprising to see them become respectable gentlemen or rich landowners after only a short time...

ed good opportunities for gatherings, gossip, and slander; the *tonsor* (barber) was always aware of everything happening in the province and it was highly appreciated by his customers. When it was their turn, the customer sat on a stool, protected by a small handkerchief or wipe and a special shirt (*involucrum*). *Faventinus* would sharpen the iron razor on a *lamitana* (a special Spanish stone), dampening it with plentiful amounts of saliva before beginning to shave the customer's beard with the utmost caution;

60. Why were Pompeiian houses given names?

Have you ever wondered how Pompeiian houses got their strange names? In some cases, it was due

to the discovery of signs or seals inside the dwelling that allowed scholars to positively identify the family that lived in that *domus*: the *Vettii*, the *Ceii*, and *Marcus Lucretrius Fronto* are just a few examples. The so-called House of Pansa (VI 6, 1), on Via Fortuna, owned by the wealthy trader *Gnaues Alleius Nigidius Maius*, was partially rented out in 79 AD, as evidenced by a painted advertisement outside of the building. For the most part, house names were conventional and arbitrarily attributed at the time

of discovery based on a series of factors. Sometimes it was because of a decorative detail, such as with the House of Venus in the Shell which opened up onto Via dell'Abbondanza (II 3, 3) that was given its name for the mega-sized painting of the goddess located in the large garden. The House of the Golden Cupids (VI 16, 7), belonging to the *Gens Poppaea*, the family of the second wife of Nero, takes its name from the original decoration of one of the rooms. Embedded in the plaster, some glass disks were

found with golden leaf on the back of them engraved with figures of cupids. The famous House of the Faun (VI 12) is named after the bronze statuette that adorned the *impluvium*; the House of the Large Fountain on Via di Mercurio (VI 8 23) was named after the beautiful fountain of polychrome mosaics and vitreous paste that can still be admired there; and the name for the House of the Tragic Poet (VI 8, 3) came from a painting in the *tablinum* (study) representing a theatrical scene complete with actors and musicians. Sometimes the name of a dwelling came from the memory of an important visitor or the celebration of a special event. The House of the Prince of Naples (VI 15, 7), inhabited by a low-to-middle class family, was given its name because it was excavated between 1896-98 in the presence of the prince, the future king of Italy, Vittorio Emanuele III. The House of the Silver Wedding, located in an alley off Via del Vesuvio (V 2, 1), was known as 'silver wedding' in honor of the famous wedding celebrated in 1893 by the Italian royal family, Umberto and Margherita of Savoy, the same year that it was excavated. The House of the Championnet (VIII 2, 3) commemorates the brief sojourn of the Parthenopean Republic in Naples (1798-1814), when the French general conquered the city by throwing out Ferdinand IV of Bourbon and ordered that the excavations in the southern district of Pompeii be continued in the area where the House named after him was eventually discovered.

61. Two stories told in graffiti: one of *Successus*, *Iris* and *Severus* and the other of *Novellia Primigenia*

Entire stories are told on the walls of this city, stories like that of *Successus*, *Iris* and *Severus*. *Severus*, jealous of his rival and perhaps drunk after

having a few too many, carved these words on the wall of a *caupona* (tavern) in Regio VIII: "*Successus the weaver loves the tavern girl Iris, who does not care for him, but he insists she commit to him.*" On the same wall *Successus*, angry and offended by the slander, replies: "*Envious one, I will beat you harshly. Do not provoke he who is more beautiful than you, as he is a violent, powerful man.*" But *Severus*, a frequent patron at the locale, was not at all scared and disregarding the threat, replied bravely: "*I said it and I wrote it: you love Iris, who does not care for you. Severus to Successus: it is as I have written it.*" We do not know how the argument ended, but one finale, a bit fictionalized, might have been that *Successus*, publicly humiliated by the woman and his rival, moved to another area of the city. In fact, evidence for a certain *Successus*, weaver, can be found among the names on a long list of graffiti from the most important *textrina* (weaving shop) in Pompeii (there are actually about 20 in the city!) belonging to *Marcus Terentius Eudoxus* who lived on Nola Street.

Another story is also told on these walls. *Novellia Primigenia* was not a Pompeiian. She is mentioned in a section of graffiti from the House of Menander: "*At Nocera, near Porta Romana, in the Venus district, ask for Novellia Primigenia.*" At first glance, we may think that this is a reference to one of the many wealthy young girls that Pompeiian inscriptions have given us, but that is not the case. This beautiful girl from Nocera, endowed with charm and sensuality, is also spoken about in another graffito, in a completely different tone. A couplet written on a niche at Porta Nocera decribes: "*Hello, Primigenia Nocerina. I would like to be the precious stone (of the ring) that you moisten with your mouth to imprint the seal for at least an hour.*" It is the delicate wish that a lover makes to become the gemstone on *Primigenia*'s seal to be able to touch her lips to give her kisses that were otherwise impossible...

C.I.L. IV 8356
NVCERIA QVAERES AD PORTA ROMANA
IN VICO VENERIO NOVELLIAM
PRIMIGENIAM

62. Fashionable Pompeii

The attention that Pompeiians dedicated to fashion and in particular to clothing and accessories

was not very different from similar habits found in modern times! The oldest, and perhaps the first ever, item of clothing was the *subligar*, a simple strip of linen that was knotted at the waist and used to cover the lower abdomen. Women also used a strip of cloth that supported their

breasts, the so-called *mammillare* (bra). They wore a tunic over this, the basic garment used by both men and women on all occasions of public and private life. Tunics could be made from wool or flax, depending on the season, and were formed by a single rectangle open on one side, held on the shoulders by a *fibula* and tightened at the waist by a belt. Women would have used two belts, one under the breasts and one at the hips. Female tunics could have long sleeves and fall all the way to their feet, while men wore short-sleeved versions that stopped at their calves. The most common decoration added to a tunic was the *clavus*, a purple strip of cloth that fell from the shoulder to the hem of the tunic and was a sign of privilege. What did they wear on special occasions? One of the special types of tunics that existed was used at weddings: it was white, long, and closely fitted at the waist by a belt looped by a double knot that only the groom could untie, commencing their conjugal life. On their head, brides wore a red veil with a crown of myrtle. Above their tunics, men wore a toga, the most formal clothing that existed, consisting of a heavy woolen cloth draped around the body and held together at the shoulder with a *fibula*. The

toga candida, woven with specially bleached wool, was used by those who aspired to public office, and which has survived in the present in the term "candidate". The *toga prae-texta* was worn by children up to the age of 17 and by other magistrates, some priests, consuls, and and the *aedilis*. Over the toga, women wore a *stola* made of fairly heavy cloth, full of folds and decorated with an embroidered border. When matrons appeared in public, they had to cover their head with the edge of the *stola*, which became a symbol of female virtue and modesty.

63. *Arria Marcella,* a heroine from the Romantic era

The story of *Arria Marcella,* very different from stories told today, made many tears fall

during the heart of the Romantic era. It began in 1771 with the excavation of a large suburban villa just outside Porta Ercolano that had been improperly attributed to *M. Arrius Diomedes.* In the great *cryptoporticus* (a large indoor corridor), eighteen skeletons were found including one of a young woman. A gold bracelet, rings and earrings identified her as a free, wealthy young girl named *Arria Marcella*, the daughter of the owner of the villa. One particular detail of this very real person whose name was incorrect touched the excavators: the ash tak-

en from the breast of the girl had taken its shape! The precious impression was exhibited at the Herculanense Museum (Portici), where it was seen, in the mid-1800's, by Théophile Gautier. The piece of ash in which the girl's breast was imprinted inspired the imagination of the writer who published a famous novel on the subject in 1852. By today's standards, we can feel the influence of Romanticism: three French friends traveling to Naples visit the Museum of Antiquity where the petrified breast of *Arria Marcella* and the remains of the Villa of Diomedes from Pompeii are exhibited. The story of the unfortunate Pompeiian girl upsets the youth Octavian so much that he returns later that evening to the deserted ruins of the city. By night, Pompeii takes on the form it had before the catastrophe and *Holconius Rufus*, the last *duoviro* of the city, accompanies the young man to the theater. He catches sight of *Arria Marcella*, a Roman aristocrat, among the crowd and spends hours of infinite happiness with her. Unfortunately, the dream of love is interrupted by the girl's father and the spell lasts only a short time: the girl returns to being a piece of ash and a few bones, the last surviving pieces of a past world. To finish off the story in the words spoken by *Arria*, who in spite of the fact that it was a fictitious story, can still be considered fashionable: *"you are truly dead, when you are no longer loved..."*

64. Pompeiian fortifications

Did you know that you can take a stroll along the ancient city walls? It's a particularly fascinating

journey through archeology, nature and panoramic views that continues for about 5 km from Piazza Anfiteatro to the Villa of the Mysteries. And from the stories told by the walls, you get a better understanding of the six centuries of Pompeii's history before its final destruction! It was a walled city made of small soft lava blocks that already marked an area of about 66 hectares in the first half of the 6th century BC. At the beginning of the 5th century, following a technical advancement of Greek inspiration using large limestone slabs, the Pompeiians built a new "double curtain" fortification, with two parallel walls and a fill of earth and stone on the interior, following the outline of the lava terrace that the city rose up over. Towards the end of the 4th century BC, wars with neighboring populations and the spread of war machines made it necessary to reinforce the vestments, adopting a typically Italian "ramped" fortification plan with a reinforced embankment on the inside. Near the end of the 3rd century BC, in order to cope with the danger posed by Hannibal's Carthaginian army, the perimeter was further enhanced and strengthened. The last modification came in the form of the introduction of twelve guard towers in the most undefended areas such as the northern and southern sides, which increased the defensive power of the city, armed as they were with a large number of artillerymen! The danger this time came from Rome, which Pompeii had gone against when they participated in the revolt of the Italian colonies. The Pompeiian

walls were baptized in fire in 89 BC, when Silla, commander of the legions, laid siege to the city. Even today, in the vestment between Porta Ercolano and Porta Vesuvio, hundreds of craters, holes and cusps can still be seen, left behind by the impact of ballistas, catapults, and slingshots. When Pompeii became a Roman colony again, the walls gradually lost their importance and function, and during the Imperial era, some of their features were incorporated into private buildings.

65. *Pistrina* (bakeries) in Pompeii

A large number of workshops with ovens and bakeries *(pistrina)* can be found in Pompeii, evidence that

the baking industry must have been very lucrative ... We also know that former bakers like *Paquius Proculus*, baking and placing his seal on every piece of bread, had made so much money that he was named *duoviro* (main magistrate) of the city!! After the earthquake, many poor homes were transformed into productive workshops using the atrium as a stable, adapting the *triclinium* into a place for kneading, and building millstones, wash basins and large ovens for baking in the garden. In the *pistrinum* (bakery), the process also included the grinding of grain: after having been ground, it was

put into the basin and left to dry, and then the wheat was poured into mills made from lava stones, consisting of a conical bottom (called a *meta*) and an empty biconical upper part (*catillus*). On top of the upper part was placed a rotation axis driven by an axle and two protruding shafts, which crushed the grain slowly being poured into it from above. The flour was collected onto a special lead sheet with raised edges around the circular stone at the base of the mill. The grindstones (two to four in number) were placed in areas covered with large paving stones and hand-operated by slaves or with the

help of mules. The sifted flour was then kneaded by adding water, yeast and salt and transformed by the hands of skilled assistants into the characteristic shape of the loaves. The most common was the sliced version, the so-called *moretum*, a good eighty loaves of which could go into an oven at a time!! The oven where the loaves cooked, rose and turned a golden color, was built of cement equipped with a conical cap and fitted with a square smoke chamber with a vent at the top that allowed for the proper circulation of air for correct combustion. Baking good quality bread meant knowing when it was time to re-open the oven, turn the loaves around, and when to take them out - a true art that could only be achieved after years of experience!!

66. Asellina

Asellina was a clever Pompeiian entrepreneur who ran a *thermopolium* in one of the most popular spots

on Via dell'Abbondanza. At the time of its excavation, a hermetically sealed bronze boiler was found; it was one of the jars embedded in the counter used to hold hot drinks and cereals and which contained the day's earnings: 683 sesterces, a little more than the price of a mule that cost 520 sesterces. The numerous electoral inscriptions painted on the outer wall of the shop, signed by women of Eastern origin (Zmyrina, Aegle, and Maria, the so-called "aselline") attest to the fact that patronage at the locale was not solely for the refreshments... Asellina's business was the inspiration for a famous story by Guido Milanesi in 1914, who imagined that

an officer of the English Navy who had come to Pompeii would have passed the excavations at the *thermopolium* supervised by the director at the time, Matteo Della Corte. Milanesi's story recounted all the splendor and illusions of the courtesan and her helpers. Unbeknownst to the guide, the officer had put his hand into a basket full of human bones excavated at the *thermopolium* and took a fragment of an ulna away with him. From that moment on, the man who had rummaged through the history of the tragedy of the heavens fell victim to Asellina. She appeared to him in dreams in different circumstances and told him her story: she was

a former comedian, a merchant of beverages and love before falling passionately in love with a man names *Chrestus*. But the *duoviro* at the time, *Lucius Samellius*, crazy with jealousy, broke into the lovers' nest and slit his rival's throat. Asellina was only 23 years old when the man to whom she had given all her affections was taken away, and she became *"an amphora filled with bad habits for all lips to quench their thirst while her spirit remained impervious and as cold as the earth that the amphora was made of."* From that point on, the door of her shop was open to everyone, to *Mescinio Gelone, Optato Rapiano,* the magistrates and soldiers of the city, and not only them..... the officer instead was able to rid himself of Asellina's persecution only after having sent the stolen bone back to Della Corte with a check for 1000 sesterces ...

67. Water fountains

Today, just as 2000 years ago, it is possible to quench your thirst and find relief from overheating thanks to about forty

public fountains that can be found scattered across the city's neighborhoods and restored to full functionality. The fountains are the same ones that were found in ancient times filled by a capillary water supply system. The water coming from the well of the aqueduct (the *Castellum Aquae*) reached the high masonry pillars (*castella*) located at crossroads, swelling to their limit and flowing into a *fistula*, then through smaller lead branches before finally reaching the public fountains. The quadrangular basins of the fountains were made up of large basalt stone slabs and rounded edges where evidence of the corrosion produced by the numerous amphorae of ancient patrons can still be seen... The water flows from one pillar ornately decorated with bas-reliefs to another, each one different from the others!!! Generally they contain images of the gods, but there are also effigies of animals or instruments used in sacred ceremonies. At the crossroads of Via del Vesuvio and Via della Fortuna, the sculpture depicted on the pillars is that of a Silenus that is resting by leaning on a waterskin. The most famous fountain is that of Mercury, which by extension gave its name to Via di Mercurio, whose pillars are decorated with the head of the god with his typical emblem, the caduceus, a small rod with two symmetrical intertwined serpents and two wings. The fountain, located in an alley of Regio VII near Via Marina, is one of the rare examples of a basin made with marble slabs and a pillar decorated with a rooster, which resulted in the street being named Vicolo del Gallo!

68. Julia Felix

Near the gym could be found the 'Hotel' run by Julia Felix, whose large house was plundered by thieves in 1755 looking for

art treasures, and re-excavated nearly 200 years later by Amedeo Maiuri. That the building was owned by *Julia Felix* is confirmed by writing on the exterior wall of the building. *"At the property of Julia Felix, daughter of Spurius, a bathroom worthy of the goddess Venus and suitable for high-class patrons, shops, mezzanine floors and coteries will be offered for rent from the next Ides of August (the thirteenth day of the month) until the same date has passed six times, that is, for five consecutive years."* This astute lady had thought of the idea of renting out some of the many unnecessary areas in her house especially after the ruinous earthquake of 62 AD had hit the city so hard, putting many of the well-loved bath complexes out of business. *Julia Felix*, with a mind for business, had hurriedly equipped her big house with wonderful spa baths designed for a particular audience and also built a richly decorated porch and a pergola, various shops and quarters for as many people as possible after the disaster, making a fortune ... Over the years, many people have left their mark in the graffiti of that great home. A fair number of these were part of the association of young Pompeiians that went to the Gymnasium there outfitted as it

was with all the equipment necessary for gymgoers. Some were free citizens from good families, some were of more humble backgrounds and practiced trades, and a certain *Abitus* left evidence showing that he participated in games at Nocera on April 21 of a year that cannot be established. Even couples came to find entertainment at the ancient hotel, including *Scutularius* (a manufacturer of dishes) with a certain woman named Africana ... There was no lack of slackers, as an anonymous censor reports to us: *"You hosted the innkeeper, the ceramicist, the deli-shop owner, the baker, the farmer, the bronze seller, the pawn shop owner, and now you have come back to be with the potter. If you decide to start opening your doors to women, you'll have exhausted all your employment opportunities."*

69. Scribbles, drawings and caricatures

Liberally taken from an excerpt written in 1955 by Amedeo Maiuri in *"Pompei ed Ercolano tra case ed abitanti"*.

Pompeii's humanity lets its countless voices echo once again from every corner of the city, with its anonymous crowd of slaves, freedmen, merchants, craftsmen and even the loud shouts of boys racing through the streets or intent on writing messages on the dirty walls of the houses. A real practice ground for artists was offered by the House of the Cryptoporticus (I 6, 12), a luxurious dwelling with a large underground tunnel that at one time was outlined by discreet light streaming from above via skylights, a series of large painted herms and a collection of paintings including a large scene from the Iliad illustrated from the imagination of a painter ... Within the beautiful walls of these corridors,

perhaps on a very rainy day, the children of freedmen found refuge and, with a sharpened nail, gave free expression to their graphic exercises. The smallest of the group would have been about 7 years old, judging by the height of the graffiti, the author of the drawing of a small boat with a sail like an inflated balloon and two four-legged creatures nearby that were probably supposed to have been horses but seemed more like two large sheep. The rest of the wall drawn on by even the tallest of the children was full of animals: bulls, deer, wild boars and buffaloes, a reminder of the *venationes* (animal hunts) that took place in the Pompeian amphitheater and that the children enjoyed so much ...

C.I.L. IV 9226

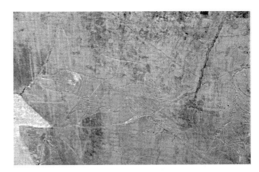

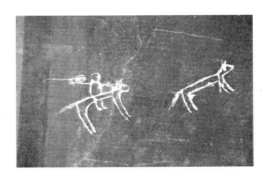

The large open air canvas offered by the walls on the street was dedicated to etched drawings of humorous caricatures of masters, an indication of the sly craftiness of slaves and freedmen in a "banter" that no one had really invented. At the entrance of the House of *Marcus Lucretius Fronto* (V, 4), graffiti is scratched into the glittering mirror of the plaster showing the disrespectful "self-portraits" of the masters. It showed the scowling face of a woman with the long forehead and short nose of a snarling dog and a virile face with a huge chin and a long, punchy nose. Similar types of images were also found on the dark red wall of the atrium of the Villa of the Mysteries where a firm hand had created the eloquent portrait of the *dominus* (master, called *Rufus*), with a bald head, fat face, and large, ruddy nose ...

70. Doctors in Pompeii

Poor *Rufus* had a severe toothache, he was suffering a lot but did not want to take any medicine because he did not

trust doctors. Which doctor was *Rufus* referring to with this serious lack of appreciation written on the walls of the city? The names of the only doctors we know of were *P. Terentius Celadus*, who was actually always spoken highly of and *A. Pumponios Magonius*, but there were surely many others in Pompeii. One of them was the owner of the House of the Surgeon (VI 1, 19), given its name because of the discovery of a series of surgical instruments, one of the most precious sets of evidence ever discovered for ancient medicine, including instruments of all kinds, well forged in bronze, iron and even steel! It contained chisels, scalpels, forceps, silver and bone needles, syringes, hooks with long handles, metal rods

usable as probes, braces, tweezers of various shapes, cautering irons, levers, and saws ... The graffiti written about the results of the various types of medical work done was not always comforting and some diseases were cured by following a certain logical set of cures: fasting, lice, dieting, and taking syringes. If you had a stomachache, a goose feather would cause vomiting. Hemorrhoids were cured by passing the patient over a brazier containing turtle shells immersed in cedar oil. If the remedy was not effective, a patient's veins were cut and sutured. Broken bones and fractures were repaired with great skill. Cataracts could be removed and doctors dared to perform complex internal operations. Most of the time the patients died and physicians were forced to run away from the city to save themselves from the anger of the patients' relatives. Of course, teeth were also pulled out, but a lack of hygiene often caused terrible infections. For one guy, it was written that after a dental extraction, he did not die, but remained blind. Poor *Rufus* was not wrong to be so cautious: considering certain results from operations, his fear was well justified!!!

71. *Marcus Nonius Campanus*

A soldier in the eighth Praetorian cohort, *Marcus Nonius Campanus* was a veteran who arrived along with many others

at the new Roman colony of Pompeii after 80 BC. The new colony was called "*Cornelia Veneria Pompeianorum*" in honor of Silla, the winner who had quelled the rebellion of the city, belonging to the *gens Cornelia* and the goddess Venus, the patron saint of Pompeii for as long as anyone could remember ... With the hoard he had earned, he rented a small shop at the intersection of Via degli Augustali and Via del Lupanare, connected to the atrium of the large house of his fellow soldier, centurion *Marcus Cesius Blandus*, who showed off his military insignia in the mosaic of the *tablinum*. Perhaps to earn a little more money,

Le Cordonnier romain (page 120).

Nonius Campanus spent his days at the shop and also acted a doorman (*ostiarius*) for *Blandus*. The popular area was densely populated, busy and full of people at all times, a great location for a shoemaker's shop! *Sutor* is the name given to *Marcus Nonius Campanus* on an inscription on the large marble table at the center of the room which held his work equipment: two lunar-shaped knives, nine chisels with iron handles, two hooks to stretch the leather, a pincushion, three bronze needles, two black shiny jars and a pair of curved scissors. With these tools, the shoemaker could repair all types of Pompeiian footwear, sandals, sandals tied around the ankles with leather cords, leather *crepidae* (soles) held on by a lace passed through the eyelets, shoe-boots with crossed laces and ivory buckles, *caligae* boots with very thick soles or the beautiful white sandals that only noble ladies wore!! *Nonius* often also had to work 'on the fly' as sometimes a carriage would stop in front of his shop blocking the traffic and give him a sandal to fix in a hurry: a few taps made cleverly on the nail and the sandal was just like new!!

72. At the House of *Quintus Poppaeus Secundus*

Liberally taken from an excerpt written in 1955 by then Superintendent of Pompeii, Amedeo Maiuri, in *"Pompei ed Ercolano tra case ed abitanti"*.

That fateful day of August 24th, 79 AD, was at the height of the summer, one of those hot days on which, just like today, the streets and roofs of Pompeii were heated by the sun. The water from the Mt. Vesuvius reservoir came to a halt in the southern districts, the old pipes had been damaged by the earthquake and not yet replaced. Men in the town had gone to the villa on the hills of Stabia or on the Sorrento coast, leaving the large urban dwellings to the *procurator*, the freedman at the head of the family of servants. This would also have been the case for the nobleman *Quintus Poppaeus*, owner of the magnificent "House of Menander (I 10, 4)", developed and expanded at the expense of the nearby houses, with two areas, one for the master and his family and the other for servants, a library, and a luxurious spa area ... The house had been damaged by the earthquake and they were just repainting the walls of the atrium with episodes of the Trojan War to fit the taste of the refined owner ... In that bustle of servants and workers, *Quintus Poppaeus* came up with the idea to hide his precious silverware in a closed box in the narrow basement, bolting the door securely. 115 plates, worked in fine

silver (weighing 24 kg), a jewelry box made of solid gold and coins worth 1,423 sesterces! But then that infernal storm began to fall on the house, a rain of ash and lava fragments from an unknown sky suddenly made of fire and stone. The bodies of the twelve workmen intent on the house's restoration were found near the entrance trying to make a desperate attempt to escape. During the absence of the inhabitants, the *procurator*, faithful to his master, had remained at his place in the cubicle where he watched the comings and goings of the servants, making notes on the produce and amphorae entering the large house, as well as organizing the workers, peasants, sommelier, stable boys, bakers, and cooks ... And this was how the excavators found the skeleton on the finely worked bed on a December morning in 1930, next to the bronze seal with his name on the side, *Quintus Eros Poppaeus.*

73. Of love, death, and other nonsense

Echoes of poetic feelings resonate from the House of Lovers (I 10, 11)
on Via dell'Abbondanza, which are said to

have belonged to *Claudius Eulogus.*
An inspired hand wrote a refined
verse in one of the squares of the
portico: *"lovers, like bees, lead a life
as sweet as honey"* with all the sweet-
ness and tenderness of a love that
can turn even the most skeptical
into dreamers ... But a word written below this verse almost breaks
the spell: *"Vellem!"*, or *"I wish that's
how it was."* The House of the Sacerdos Amandus (I 7, 7) did not leave
its mark so much for its rich decorations but rather for the moving
story of the nine people, both adults
and children, who made up the large
family (so many of them in such a
small house!) Along with the fact
that they were found all together
embracing one another by the door.
On the walls of one of the rooms,
drawings engraved with a nail by a
childish hand can still be seen, perhaps made by one of the children
found. They show a date palm, the
name *Amandus*, the name of the beloved father who could not save the
baby from death. *P. Cornelius Tages*
must also be remembered because of

his strange use of a precious statue,
a bronze Ephebus that was the inspiration for the name of the home
(I 7, 10), a masterpiece inspired by

AMANTES VT APES VITAM ELLITA DVLCEM

a Greek original from the middle of the 5th century BC. It was a precious item and must have cost a lot of money!! But even if *Cornelius Tages* did not lack the means (as the magnificent house also shows), he certainly lacked taste: he transformed the precious object into a lamp holder to hang over the convivial table of his garden, enough to make any art connoisseur shiver! The Ephebus was found wrapped in linen cloths which the owner had used to try to defend it against the danger of that famous night ...

74. *Marcus Epidius Sabinus, juris doctor* (doctor of law)

The first thing you notice in front of the house of exceptional distinction is the high threshold (about 1.50 m) when entering the house

through the main door. Even the atrium with its 16 columns stretching high into the sky is one of the grandest to be found in Pompeii. In this house, IX 1, 22, lived *M. Epidius Sabinus*, universally known throughout the city as *iuris doctor*, an expert in legal advice. The influence of *Epidius Sabinus* is also evident from the number of electoral inscriptions that cover the façade of his home and that of his neighbors, a truly enthusiastic ode to him that acclaims him, even though he was still young, as *duoviro* of Pompeii! Within the sumptuous dwelling, there was an elegant *lararium* in the shape of a temple, dedicated, as reported by the inscription engraved on the marble, both to the household gods (the Lari) as well as the *gens* of Sabinus' father, *Marcus Epidius Rufus*, on the part of two families of freedmen. The two slaves that were given their freedom by their beloved patron had expressed their gratitude and affection by dedicating the *lararium* to the *gens* of the head of household! Roman tradition was to dedicate a tribute to the *Genius*, often symbolized by a snake heading towards the altar filled with an egg and some fruit, votive offerings painted underneath the image

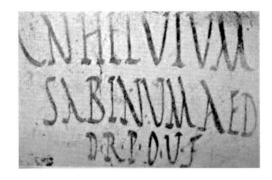

of the household gods, with two youths offering libations. But let's return to *Epidius Sabinus*. On the façade of the block in front of the house can be read. *"I ask you all to elect M. E. Sabinus. He is worthy of this office and, by decision of the Holy Judge, Suedius Clemens, has been called on to be the public defender of the Republic, with the consent of the council of the decurions. You should also elect him because he is worthy of administering public affairs on the basis of his merits and his honesty, writes the scriptwriter Sabinus, who is also convinced."* A true ode of admiration for this citizen, not only by the council of decurions, the highest expression of popular opinion had made their voice heard, but also by the magistrate, *Suedius Clemens*, representative of the Emperor's power!

75. The House of *Casca Longus*

This story begins in Rome, *caput mundi* (capital of the world) far more then than it is now. The protagonist of the story is *Publius Servilius Casca (Longus),*

no less than one of Gaius Julius Caesar's assassins, killed on March 15, 44 BC. Indeed, according to the accounts from the time, it was *Casca Longus* who made the first blow, attacking Caesar from behind and wounding his neck. At this point, you will already be wondering what *Casca Longus* has to do with Pompeii. The answer is that a

dwelling found at number 11 in Regio I, Building 6, bears this name. No one had ever thought that the nobleman *Casca Longus* had lived in such a small provincial town like Pompeii, and I will now tell you how the story went. In the chaos after the death of Caesar, *Casca Longus* was suddenly appointed as tribune of the plebeians,

but in a rapid turnaround typical of the political scene, he went from being a "savior of the republic" together with the other conspirators, to being a public enemy. He was the target of persecution organized by Octavius (the future Augustus) against all the perpetrators of Caesar's death and *Casca Longus* was banned, deprived of office and forced to flee to the east, where he committed suicide in 42 AD following defeat in the Battle of Philippi at Macedonia. His property and assets were confiscated and sent to public auction. Among his belongings, there must have been a circular marble table decorated with three lion-headed legs bearing his name "*P. Casca Long(us)*". The table, passing through a series of owners, was found decades later among the furnishings of the rich owner of this Pompeiian home, used as a table in the dining area that usually decorated one side of the *impluvium*. That the owner was an attentive collector of valuable objects is also shown by the rest of the furnishings found in the house, including a statuette of Apollo with a fawn made in Archaic style, echoing the type created by the Greek artist Canachos in the second half of the 4th century BC for the famous Sanctuary of Apollo Didyma in Asia Minor. Not to mention the frescoes in the atrium of the house, decorated with paintings of subjects inspired by the works of Euripides and Menander...

76. The House of the Vettii

The *Vettii* brothers, *Restitutus* and *Conviva*, rich freedmen, were the owners of this large home. After the earthquake,

they were one of the very few able to completely restore the building, hiring the best artists in the city to plaster the walls. Beside the front door, they commissioned an image of *Priapus*, a country god, shown standing up resting his gigantic member, a timeless symbol of luck, on the plate of a set of scales, balanced by a bag full of money, the result of his benevolence. Of the crushed and deformed atrium, only two arches survived, guardians of a wealth of information that unfortunately we do not know about, but that we find in Pompeii only

in the homes of the rich. The highlight of the house was the garden, rich with flowers and plants and completely restored, perhaps the most beautiful in Pompeii: marble and bronze sculptures, artistically crafted tables, fountains and pools filled with precious statuettes could be seen everywhere. One of the rooms that opened up onto this wonder contained frescoes of cupids busily working at crafts and businesses found in Pompeii. The most refined image is that of the harvest scene: the picking, pressing, full vats, pouring of the wine and the centerpiece of Bacchus and Arianna. Who knows if the riches of the *Vettii* were due to the production of wine: in their well-stocked wine cellar, amphorae were found containing clearly valuable wine, as evidenced by the inscriptions painted on the vessels with the indication of the quality, origin and date of production ... A true DOC (guaranteed origin) ... The house also contained a well-preserved *lararium*, the familiar Genius between the two dancing Lari has the features of the Emperor Nero in a toga ... Who knows if maybe it was a way to feel more equal to the aristocratic relatives of *Poppaea* from the House of Menander...

77. Marcus Epidius Hymenaeus, the Moralist

M. Epidius Hymenaeus, owner of House III 4, 2-3 has gone down in history as a "moralist." His home was located

between Via dell'Abbondanza and Via di Nocera. He was a small-sized merchant and producer of wine and terracotta pots. In his house, he built a small, attractive room, a *triclinium* suitable for guests and friends, in which the three beds and the dining area at the center were still well preserved. On the black background of the three walls, the decoration was unusual: painted in white over a few pecking birds and written in poetic form were the three rules that the master wanted observed in his home and that gave him his nickname. The first was of a practical nature: *"Wash your feet with water and after they are wet, a slave will dry them: a spread covers the bed so that we do not dirty our linens."* Another was about ethics: *"Keep your lecherous gaze and languid eyes away from the wives of others; your mouth preserves your modesty."* The final was an invitation to have good manners: *"Abstain from anger and contempt if you can; otherwise, go to your own house."* This Moralist was a good man, serious and reserved, and very attentive to the rules on how to live, but also a little bit superstitious!! He had a large earthenware rooster commissioned on the façade of his house that had two huge phalluses in place of its head and tail! In Pompeii, everyone knew that this sign of fertility and love was the most effective talisman against bad luck!

78. Pious, modest, frugal, and chaste...

"Pious, moral, frugal, and chaste, a housewife that stayed at home and spun wool". This is what was written on the grave of an ideal

wife and mother. In Pompeii, we know the names, faces, and stories of many women who lived their lives by lavishing all their attention on their husband, children, and home. There is in a true gallery of portraits. *Rustica*, the grouchy wife of *Caecilius Jucundus*: she had a strong character but also all of the qualities necessary to manage the family heritage wisely. Otherwise, how would her husband have accumulated so much wealth that he could buy a large piece of property, a rustic villa in the suburbs of Pompeii located in modern day Boscoreale? *Cassia*, the wife of *Saturninus*, who lived in the House of the Faun (VI 12, 25) on that tragic day in 79 AD had prepared a special lunch, but the two chickens in the kitchen did not have time to cook; she was found in the atrium of the house having tried desperately to escape. *Blesia*, the wife of *Postumius Modestus*, loved luxury and comfort. The peristyle in her house on Via dell'Abbondanza (VII 4, 4) was enriched with pools and fountains. A beautiful golden necklace with amulets and pendants was found around her neck. *Quartilla*, the wife of the architect *Appius Gratius*, was modest and satisfied with her simple bronze brooches, even if she

had a mosaic signed by the famous *musivarius* (mosaic worker) Felix in her beautiful house (IX 6, 5). *Equitia*, the wife of the carpenter *Volusius Juvencus* (I 10, 7): she had her husband make her son a toy, a 4-wheeled wooden cart. *Claudia*, the wife of *Trebius Valens* (III 2, 1) lived surrounded by the wealth of her rich husband and everyone was jealous of her, so that even the poor slave *Tirsa* wrote on a wall of the house: *"O Valens, if only I were your lady!"* Melissa, Marcellus' wife (IX 2, 26): her husband had won the election as an *aedilis* and to celebrate the event had given her a gold necklace, 2 meters and 55 centimeters long, a jewel that few women in Pompeii could afford!!!

79. "*Quota hora est?*" What time is it?

Eumachia, Caecilius Jucundus, Trebius Valens, Julia Felix, and the *duoviro Holconius Rufus,* everyone in Pompeii

told time by raising their eyes to the sky and observing the sun's position ... In the *Forum*, a town crier shouted out the hours on a solar clock found in the temple of Apollo near the altar steps: it was supported by a marble column and was commissioned by the *duoviri L. Sepurnius* and *M. Erennius*. In the basilica, an hourglass was used during the processes to measure the passage of time: judges and lawyers' speeches could not last longer than 20 minutes. The day was divided into 24 hours, 12 during the day and 12 at night. As the weather varied during different seasons and the amount of time between dawn and sunset changed, in the winter, daytime hours lasted 45 minutes, and nighttime hours an hour and a quarter; during the summer, it was vice versa. Day and night were actually further divided into 4 parts of 3 hours each, the *vigiliae* (Vigils), which people then adjusted their daily movements to. They used a solar clock, an hourglass, some longer hours and some shorter hours, daytime *vigiliae* and nighttime *vigiliae* and no one probably ever knew exactly what time it was!!! But why would they have needed to? In the *Forum*, the town crier announced aloud when

proceedings would begin, when the popular assembly would take place, when orators from the tribune would speak during election campaigns or when voting would begin. Other town criers wandered through the streets of the city and provided accurate news broadcasting the start times of shows and the market days. The bells that were found in many houses served to awaken inhabitants at dawn when the servants began cleaning the rooms. Even the owner got up early, a line of customers waiting for him on his doorstep with shopping bags to be filled, according to their means, by the servant in charge. The master, after checking the accounts and merchandise, hur-

ried off to the Forum: the streets were crowded, the shops opened up, the merchants went to the Forum and the people came and went. After a midday snack, there was a long break at the baths and the *coena* (dinner) during the early hours of sunset, people went to bed early. The streets were so dark that those who came home late from dinners would have to be accompanied by slaves carrying lanterns. Was it a happy life? The average Pompeiian probably did not even ask themselves that, accepting both the good and bad parts of life, as a unknown hand wrote on the wall of the house: *"Nothing can last forever."*

Finito di stampare nel mese di maggio 2018
Per «L'ERMA» di BRETSCHNEIDER
da Services4Media - Viale Caduti di Nassiriya, 39, 70124 Bari

II ristampa Luglio 2022